THE PENGUIN C

FOUNDER EDITOR (1944-

PRESENT EDITORS

Betty Radice and Robert Baldick

THE PENGUIN CLASSICS
THE MOST RECENT VOLUMES

★

GOWER
Confessio Amantis · *Terence Tiller*

JOINVILLE and **VILLEHARDOUIN**
Chronicles of the Crusades · *M. R. B. Shaw*

EURIPIDES
Medea and Other Plays · *Philip Vellacott*

BERNAL DÍAZ
The Conquest of New Spain · *J. M. Cohen*

RACINE
Phaedra and Other Plays · *John Cairncross*

SALLUST
The Jugurthine War and the Conspiracy of Catiline
S. A. Handford

VOLTAIRE
Zadig and L'Ingénu · *John Butt*

LAO TZU
Tao Te Ching · *D. C. Lau*

BEAUMARCHAIS
The Barber of Seville and The Marriage of Figaro
John Wood

BENJAMIN CONSTANT
Adolphe · *L. W. Tancock*

★

*For a complete list of books available please write to Penguin Books
whose address can be found on the back of the title page*

69278

LUCRETIUS

ON THE NATURE OF THE
UNIVERSE

*

TRANSLATED
AND WITH AN INTRODUCTION
BY RONALD LATHAM

*

PENGUIN BOOKS
BALTIMORE · MARYLAND

PRAIRIE STATE COLLEGE
LEARNING CENTER

Penguin Books Ltd, Harmondsworth, Middlesex, England
Penguin Books Inc., 3300 Clipper Mill Road, Baltimore 11, Md, U.S.A.
Penguin Books Pty Ltd, Ringwood,
Victoria, Australia

—

This translation first published 1951
Reprinted 1952, 1955, 1957, 1958, 1959, 1960, 1961, 1962, 1963, 1964

—

Copyright © Ronald Latham, 1951

—

Made and printed in Great Britain
by The Whitefriars Press Ltd
London and Tonbridge
Set in Monotype Perpetua

This book is sold subject to the condition
that it shall not, by way of trade, be lent,
re-sold, hired out, or otherwise disposed
of without the publisher's consent,
in any form of binding or cover
other than that in which
it is published

CONTENTS

MORTALIBUS
AEGRIS

INTRODUCTION

*

IF you woke up one morning to discover that some miracle had
transported you to Athens in the early years of the third century
B.C., you would find yourself in a social and spiritual atmosphere
not altogether unfamiliar. The political ideals of the city-state –
liberty, democracy, national self-sufficiency – had lost their appeal
in a world dominated by large-scale despotisms and shaken by
economic crises and social unrest. The old gods retained their
temples and their sacrifices, but had ceased to inspire a living faith.
The master minds of the preceding century, Plato and Aristotle,
seemed to have no message for the rising generation – no medicine
for the prevailing mood of disillusionment, scepticism, and
fatalism.

In this setting, if you are one of those who believe that civilization with all its conventional values has been debunked, you would
find congenial company among the followers of Diogenes the
Cynic, whose simple and self-centred life in the tub had demonstrated how many valued assets of mind and body it is possible to
do without. If you are a puzzled seeker after the Unknown God,
you would find yourself no less at home among the Stoics, the
devout company who gathered in the Painted Portico to hear that
impassioned prophet Zeno of Cyprus proclaim his doctrine of
submission to an all-wise Providence. And, if you are by temperament a rationalist, ready to welcome the assurance that modern
science has disposed, once and for all, of the fairy-tales that
pleased our grandparents and the bogeys that frightened them,
then sooner or later you would find your way to that peaceful
garden where Epicurus preached his gospel of salvation by
common sense.

The Epicurean gospel was spread by zealous missionaries
throughout the Greek world, and a century or so after the Master's
death it was preached within the walls of all-conquering Rome

(175 B.C.). The Roman aristocracy, whose system was founded on authority and tradition, expelled these first apostles as dangerously subversive. But a century later, with the spread of Greek culture and the decay of traditional standards among the educated classes at Rome, the new doctrine had made many converts. In particular, it impinged with all the force of a divine revelation on the sensitive soul of one Roman citizen, by name Titus Lucretius Carus, who happened also to be one of the world's supremely great poets. And Lucretius, like a true Epicurean, turned aside from the path of politics and war which was the normal career of the Roman gentleman and devoted his life to an exposition of his Master's teaching.

In form, the poem is addressed to Gaius Memmius, an eminent Roman statesman whose career is no great testimony to the moral efficacy of Epicurean doctrine. In fact, Lucretius was addressing a wider audience in the hope that, tempted by 'the sweet honey of the Muses' (I 947), they would 'swallow the bitter draught' of his doctrine and so find peace. Not least, he was addressing us. In the course of 2,000 years of scientific and religious experience, some articles of his creed have become incredible, some have become commonplace. But we can still feel the impulsive force of his tremendous personal conviction, even if at times our chief impulse may be to counter his arguments and urge him to think again. There is no ancient writer who speaks more directly to the modern reader.

Apart from this poem, Lucretius is scarcely more than a name. He must have been born soon after 100 B.C., on the eve of the murderous civil war between the aristocrat Sulla and the Popular leader Marius. He was probably already dead when his poem was given to the world about 55 B.C., during the uneasy lull that preceded the recrudescence of civil war under Pompey and Cæsar.[1] It is doubtful what truth, if any, lies behind the traditional story

1. His reference almost at the end of the poem to the British climate (VI 1106) prompts the question whether he may have lived to hear a report of Caesar's expedition of 55 B.C., possibly from Quintus Cicero, who was Caesar's lieutenant and was probably a friend of the poet.

(immortalized by Tennyson) that he died by his own hand after being driven mad by a love philtre. Certainly, there are omissions and loose ends, especially in the later books, which suggest that the author had not time to complete the work of revision. Few, however, will readily accept the statement of the ancient biographer that this masterpiece of logical coherence was created by a madman in his 'lucid intervals'. Readers are more likely to echo the surprise implied in the comment of his first critic, Cicero, in a letter to his brother Quintus (Feb., 54 B.C.), that it was written 'with many high-lights of genius, *but* with much art'. To the poet himself, the purple patches of lyric beauty and intensity were of secondary importance: they were woven with great care into the pattern of an exceedingly tough fabric.

Lucretius failed in his purpose. As a poet he has had no lack of admirers. From Virgil onwards they have been ready enough to sip the honey of his verse. But comparatively few were prepared to profit by his unpalatable physic. Under the Roman Empire there were many avowed Epicureans; but they were interested in the Master's tolerant and easy-going morality rather than its scientific and philosophic foundations. To the Christians the whole system was of course anathema, though some of the Fathers found Lucretius a useful arsenal of ammunition against the Pagan gods. From the collapse of Classical civilization, only one battered manuscript of the poem was preserved to form the basis of all existing copies. In the Renaissance Lucretius was rediscovered as a poet; but it is only since the seventeenth century, when the rationalizing French priest Gassendi advanced an atomic theory based on his teaching, that Epicureanism has been treated with respect as a serious attempt to explain the physical universe. As recently as 1918, when a defence of materialism by H. Woods appeared under the Lucretian title *On the Nature of Things*, it was possible to argue that with minor modifications Lucretius' teaching could be reconciled with the latest findings of modern science. To-day, for better or for worse, the atom has been well and truly split, and it looks as though much of the mechanical materialism of the eighteenth and nineteenth centuries has been shattered with

it. But this change (which may not be permanent) in the content
of current scientific theories does not lessen the value of Lucretius'
poem as a poet's exposition of the scientific outlook – or at least
of an outlook which has inspired much of the most fruitful work
in the field of the natural sciences. Lucretius was one of the
relatively small number who have accepted the evidence of the
senses at its face value – have dismissed metaphysical abstractions,
Divine Providence and the immortal soul as vain illusions – and at
the same time have found ample grounds for wonder and joy in
the perceptible universe and the omnipotent and omnipresent
working of natural law. The present translator had the pleasure
of introducing Lucretius to a scientific worker who had felt
constrained to accept this materialist view at any rate as a working
hypothesis. In his enthusiastic response to the Lucretian vision of
the universe it was possible to see a reflexion (an 'image', as
Lucretius would have called it) of the poet's own reaction to the
teaching of Epicurus.

In essence Epicureanism is the simplest of all philosophies – so
simple that it is hard to find words for it in a language that teems
with names for objects which Epicurus believed to be non-existent.
He believed that all knowledge is derived from the senses (cf.
Lucretius I 422–25, etc.). Things are exactly as they appear to be
to our senses, or rather as they would appear to be if our senses
were slightly more acute. Material objects are perceived. Therefore they exist. When the wind blows through the tree tops, we
perceive that the branches toss; but the wind itself is not perceived (I 271–97). Must we then suppose that it is something
different in kind from the things we do perceive? Not at all. We
can imagine it (i.e. form an image of it) as a stream of material
particles, like motes in a sunbeam (II 126) but even smaller,
knocking against the boughs. By similar reasoning Epicurus sought
to explain everything we perceive without positing the existence
of anything other than material objects and the space in which they
move, which is simply the absence of material objects. From this
primary assumption everything else follows. Astronomers are
wrong in supposing the moon to be something other than that

shining disc (or part-disc) whose image strikes on our eyes (V 577-78, etc.). Psychologists are wrong in thinking that the mind is anything other than an assemblage of very mobile particles that easily group themselves into patterns or images in conformity with other images that impinge upon them from outside objects (see below, pp. 17-18). Moralists are wrong in supposing that anything can be good except those pleasurable sensations (or movements of the mind atoms) which the senses themselves immediately perceive to be good (II 258, 966; VI 26, etc.). We are all wrong when we delude ourselves with dreams, or torment ourselves with nightmares, of invisible powers interfering to upset the regular and determinate working of the perceptible universe (V 76-90, etc.).

Most of the Epicurean dogmas, however startling they may appear at first sight, can be readily grasped as attempts to apply this central principle in the absence of microscopes or other aids to sense-perception and of any technique for testing hypotheses by practical experiment. As expounded by Lucretius, they fit easily into place with no more explanation than he himself supplies. Of course every dogma has a history. The historically minded reader will be intrigued to catch the echoes of forgotten controversies – a tirade against the Stoic hero Hercules or an elephantine mockery of Anaxagoras for a theory that he probably never held. He will trace the debt of Epicurus to the fifth-century atomists, Leucippus and Democritus, and speculate how far these in their turn were trying to reconcile the individualist tendencies of the Ionians with the totalitarianism of the Western Greeks. But it is possible to know nothing of these things and still to understand and enjoy Lucretius. For these problems lie below the surface; and Epicurus was consciously and deliberately superficial. He believed that truth was not at the bottom of the well, but very near the surface, scarcely veiled in the outward appearance of things. For this reason his language was pictorial, and in the hands of a poet easily became picturesque. For the same reason he was remarkably free from the tyranny of words and the disguised assumptions implied in them. He was less inclined than most philosophers to regard the common beliefs of his contemporaries as universal truths. Plato and Aristotle were doubtless far more profound thinkers; but they are unmistakably dated as fourth-century Greeks, thinking in terms of Hellene and Barbarian, citizen and alien, free man and slave. For Epicurus, these distinctions which eluded the senses were not part of the essence of man, but mere accidents (I 455–58).

In one notable particular, Epicurus failed to escape the limitations of his age. He accepted the word 'god' (in the Classical, not the Christian, sense) as the name of an object. He could not believe that those stately figures that caught his eye at every street corner, that were stamped on every coin and painted on every jar, were 'images' that had formed themselves in the mind atoms of the original artists without pressure from without. They must correspond to some external object. So he found a home for the blessed Olympians far away from human affairs, in the interspaces between the worlds (II 1090–1104; III 18–24; V 146–173, etc.), and worshipped them as models of felicity in the happy assurance that they were as impotent as they were indifferent.

In one particular, again, Epicurus indulged in a metaphysical subtlety foreign to the spirit of his materialist doctrine. As a moralist, he believed in free will. If the movements of the atoms were absolutely determined, as Democritus had taught, it seemed to him that all human actions must be equally determinate. Therefore the atoms must swerve, very rarely and very little, from the paths ordained for them by nature (II 216–93). To contemporaries this seemed an absurd notion. We may doubt whether it was really relevant to the moral question at issue. But it was the one concession in a dogmatic system to that element of the inexplicable and unpredictable in nature which some modern physicists have been driven to acknowledge by a somewhat similar concession.

This then was the raw material of Lucretius' poem. And, because he was a disciple first and a poet second, he assigned a place in the plan to every jot of the Master's teaching, however dull or trivial. He must deal as painstakingly with knotty problems of optics or meteorology as with the inspiring topic of human progress and the origin of civilization. He might add a little honey of his own, but he would not alter the prescription. Only, as a poet, he could not help colouring the mixture with the lights and shades of his own strongly marked personality.

Like Epicurus, Lucretius was an enemy of 'religion' – all the more so because the omens and taboos that made up the substance of Roman *religio*[2] were even more obviously designed than Greek mythology to terrorize and bewilder. He accepted the shadowy gods of Epicurus, but was not interested in them. He reserved his religious emotions for an impersonal Nature, invoked at the opening of the poem under the conventional guise of Venus. He found Nature blind, soulless and purposeless, but with a breath-taking beauty and majesty that could dispense with any personal attributes.

Above all, Lucretius took delight in the fruitfulness of Nature. With this went, not unnaturally, a deep appreciation of domestic happiness (III 894–96), and an antipathy to the barren cult of 'love' as glorified by contemporary poets. This, like the romantic love of the troubadours, was entirely dissociated from marriage. But, unlike romantic love, it was not praised as an incentive to heroic deeds. It was a sentiment indulged in for its own sake. And as such it was condemned by Lucretius (IV 1058–1191), from the Epicurean standpoint, with a bitterness never excelled by the sternest of Puritans.

Epicurus disapproved of intense pleasure because of the inevitable reaction. His goal was tranquillity; and, since he seems to have enjoyed an equable temperament, he may have come near to attaining it. Lucretius did not. By temperament he was more poet than philosopher, a man of moods. He may have intended to end his poem on a more cheerful and Epicurean note than that struck by the actual conclusion of the text (VI 1138–1286) – a highly coloured version of Thucydides' grim account of the plague

2. This was a neutral term, neither good nor evil. Since it normally excluded some essential elements of our word 'religion' (e.g. righteous conduct and the sense of mystic communion), it has generally been translated here as 'superstition'; but in itself it did not convey the derogatory implications of *superstitio* and its English derivative.

of 430 B.C. at Athens. But a man so sensitive to human suffering must have found himself at best a lonely figure among his tough contemporaries. He could sympathize with Nature. But, in that age of mad ambition and murderous class-war (I 29–43; III 59–86), he found it hard to sympathize with his fellow men. He was oppressed at times (as Epicurus, apparently, was not) by the unfriendliness of the world (II 573–80; V 195–234) and the thought of its impending dissolution (II 1150–74; V 91–109; VI 596–607). We may suspect that the childish terrors, of which he speaks so feelingly (II 55–8, etc.), were not so much banished by his philosophy as diverted into other channels. Yet the great attraction of Lucretius is undoubtedly his defiant conviction that he has honestly faced these fears and trampled them underfoot – that he is, as Virgil saw him, happy in having understood the causes of things (I 78–9; III 14–40, 319–22; Virgil: *Georgics*, II 490).

For the translator the poem of Lucretius poses an awkward problem. There are indeed several English versions that admirably fulfil the purpose of aiding the student in his study of the original text. But in achieving this object they can scarcely fail to strike a reader unversed in Latin idiom as strangely contorted and at times barely intelligible. When such a reader is confronted by the sentence, 'And therefore their seats as well must be unlike our seats, fine, as their bodies are fine' (V 153–4), or 'But that you may not by chance think that after all only those idols of things wander abroad which come off from things, there are those too which are begotten of their own accord, and are formed of themselves in this sky that is called air' (IV 129–32), he may be pardoned if he decides that Lucretius is beyond his comprehension. In fact these scholarly translators (to one of whom, incidentally, I owe a deep debt of gratitude for his illuminating and exciting lectures) set themselves an impossible task. The present version was undertaken in the hope that, by abandoning all attempt to reproduce the grammatical structure of the Latin, it might prove possible to express the poet's meaning and something of his spirit without any wide departure from normal English usage.

After all, what Lucretius himself was trying to do was to convey a fundamentally simple message in direct and forcible language. Where he failed (which was not in fact very often), this was not usually due to any intrinsic complexity or abstruseness in the 'dark discoveries' (I 136) of his Master. Still less was he hampered by any personal bent towards over-subtlety or pretentiousness that might have made him unable or unwilling to express himself clearly. His main difficulty, as he fully recognized, was 'the poverty of his native speech' (I 139, 832; III 260) – the speech of a semi-barbarous people who had displayed unequalled aptitude for the arts of government and war but had so far devoted very little thought to 'the nature of the universe'. The Latin of Lucretius' day had no accepted philosophic or scientific vocabulary, and his generation had to create one for themselves on the Greek model. In this task Lucretius was handicapped by his resolve to 'honey his medicine' (I 947) by writing in the exacting medium of heroic verse. This automatically debarred him from using any of the numerous Latin words that cannot be squeezed into a hexameter. It also imposed certain literary conventions. In modelling himself on the 'immortal verses' (I 121) of Ennius, the great epic poet of the preceding century, Lucretius committed himself to a style rich in archaisms and indirect allusions ('fleecy tribes', 'vine-begotten fluid', and the like) and in striking effects of alliteration and assonance that occasionally degenerated into jingles. Obviously he found this style congenial. But his choice of it was not just a personal eccentricity. While a phrase like *mutae natantes squamigerum pecudes* (II 342–3) was not the normal Latin way of saying 'fish', it was the sort of phrase a poet of the old school was expected to use: it can scarcely have affected a contemporary Roman as a twentieth-century Englishman would be affected by 'voiceless swimming flocks of scaly ones'.

If Lucretius could achieve lucidity and dignity in the teeth of an intractable vocabulary and a stylistic convention not altogether appropriate to his purpose, they should not be beyond the reach of a relatively unfettered translator. But the latter soon discovers, not only that he is not Lucretius but that his freedom means loss

as well as gain. In writing twentieth-century English, he must
often choose between an archaic expression with pleasing associa-
tions and a baldly scientific one. The distinction was not so clear-
cut in the seventeenth century, when the adjective 'massy', for
instance, was equally at home in the languages of Milton and of
Newton. But since then poetry and science have gone different
ways, and recent attempts to reunite them have not yet been
wholly successful. So, where Lucretius could so wield his limited
vocabulary as to combine the Biblical stateliness of 'every beast
of the field after his kind eating green herb' with the scientific
precision of 'every species of herbivorous mammal', the translator
often finds it hard not to sacrifice one or the other. By injudicious
compromise he may easily sacrifice both. I have tried to steer a
middle course, but a somewhat zigzag one. My aim has been to
match passages of close reasoning with a suitably technical
terminology. In other passages, where the surging music of the
Latin has imposed on the translation an unescapable rhythmic beat,
the vivid Lucretian imagery has demanded a language more native
to verse than to scientific prose. In theory, I believe, this course
can be convincingly justified. How far I have actually succeeded in
dodging the reefs that beset it is another matter.

Lucretius naturally indulges far less freely than most Classical
poets in those mythological allusions that agreeably flattered the
intelligence of ancient readers but on modern ones are more likely
to act as an irritant. A few such passages, however, have seemed
to me sufficiently obscure to merit elucidation by a somewhat free
rendering: e.g. a literal translation of I 739 (= V 112) would be,
'those that the Pythian woman pronounces from Phoebus' tripod
and laurel', an expression that would not have puzzled any
educated reader in a society which accepted Greek mythology as
one of the main vehicles of education. There is in any case no need
to increase the mythological element in Lucretius by making him
refer to the sun as 'he' and to the moon as 'she' because the rules
of Latin grammar prevent him from doing otherwise.

Particular problems are presented by some of Lucretius' key-
words. Since his *primordia rerum* correspond to the *atomoi* of

Epicurus, I have felt justified in rendering them as 'atoms', or in some contexts as 'elements', rather than 'first-beginnings of things'. Alternative names of the atoms ('generative particles', 'seeds', etc.) have been literally translated when the context seemed to require it. For *inane* the rendering 'void' is appropriate in some settings ('the illimitable void', etc.), but as a technical term it has seemed more natural to use 'vacuum' or 'vacuity'. I have tried always to observe the distinction between (a) the infinite 'universe' (*summa rerum*); (b) the 'world' (*mundus*), including earth and sky and the 'flaming ramparts' – the outer envelope of fiery ether which feeds the heavenly bodies; and (c) the 'earth' itself (*tellus* or *terra*, both terms being sometimes restricted to 'dry land').

As is natural in a purely materialistic system, it is the physiological and psychological questions discussed in Books III and IV that make the biggest demands on author, translator and reader. When Lucretius speaks of ideas or worries as harboured in the 'breast', he is to be understood quite literally. In the breast he locates that mixture of heat, air, wind, and an unnamed fourth substance which together constitutes the source of all thought and feeling. The name *animus* or *mens*, applied to this mixture, is generally rendered as 'mind', though as the seat of emotion it corresponds equally to our notion of the 'heart': it is clear, for instance, that *miseras hominum mentes* (II 14) refers to this emotional aspect of the *animus*, while *pectora caeca* ('blind breasts') in the same line alludes to the intellectual function of perception which it ought to be performing. The same atomic mixture in a less concentrated form, interfused throughout the limbs, composes the *anima* or vital principle. Since Lucretius applies the term *anima* also to the Platonic conception (which, of course, he does not share) of an immortal self-subsistent *psyché*, the word is commonly translated 'soul'. I have tried to cover this double sense by using the more ambiguous term 'spirit' or 'vital spirit'. When the atoms of *animus* and *anima* are jostling one another in a particular way (when they have 'entered into the sensory motions'), they somehow give rise to *sensus* ('sentience') – a term that embraces both

consciousness in general and specific sensations. How the atoms
respond to the impacts of external objects and 'images' is a point
that must be left, together with other technicalities, for Lucretius
himself to explain.

It remains to note one last problem, that presented by the state
of the text, which owing to its transmission through one imperfect
channel (above, p. 9) is possibly more disfigured by gaps and
uncertainties than that of any other Latin author. I have generally
followed the latest edition of the Oxford Text, edited by Dr Cyril
Bailey (1947); but for the purposes of this version, where textual
criticism would obviously be out of place, I have occasionally
departed from it in what may appear a somewhat arbitrary fashion.
My guiding principle has been to avoid any speculative reading
that does not fit easily into the context. It is just possible, for
instance, that the MS reading *videmus Sensibus sedatum* (II 462) is
what Lucretius actually wrote, whereas Lachmann's emendation
venenumst Sensibu' sed rarum is textually far from convincing; but I
have thought it better to base my version on the latter, which
imports no new idea into the passage, rather than attempt, as
Munro does, to extract a disputable meaning out of the received
text. Where a passage can be made intelligible by the omission of
an obviously corrupt word or a corrupt or incomplete phrase
(e.g. the word *epicuri* in II 42, or the phrase *in primis pleraque dona*
in II 681), I have simply omitted it. Munro's ingenious suggestion
et ecum vi for *epicuri* in the former passage may well be right; but
there seems no point in introducing a brilliant guess into a context
whose general sense remains unaffected. Where there is an
undoubted gap in the text, I have introduced a word or two to
bridge the gulf. The substance of these brief interpolations is
always more or less implied in the context and in some cases
explicitly stated elsewhere; but, of course, the actual content of
the missing passage may have been much fuller and more striking.
    Some of the apparent incoherences in the poem have a special
interest, as they may be due not to mishaps in the transmission of
the text but to loose ends awaiting revision at the time of the

poet's death. There is for instance an undoubted element of incon-
sequence and self-contradiction about the digression on the use
of wild beasts in war (V 1308–49), in which Dr Bailey sees the
one possible support in the text for the legend of the poet's
insanity. Does this macabre scene reflect the nightmare horror of
some actual experience, presumably of the arena rather than the
battlefield? Or is it based on controversies raised by some forgotten
episode of history – some ancient parallel to the disastrous attempt
of the defenders of Panama to ward off Morgan's buccaneers by
driving stampeded cattle into their ranks? At any rate, it would
be rash to blame Lucretius for seeming lapses from lucidity that
may equally well be due to his own untimely death, to a careless
editor or copyist, or just to our present ignorance.

When all is said and done, these difficulties must not be exag-
gerated. It is not often that the general drift of an argument is in
doubt. Neither the imperfections of the text nor the inadequacy
of translation (unless the translator does his job very badly indeed)
should be an insurmountable barrier between Lucretius and the
modern reader. For the poet succeeded in making the essence of
his message so clear that it is hardly possible to misunderstand or
misrepresent it. And with Lucretius that is what matters.

September 1949   R. E. L.

SYNOPSIS

*

THIS synopsis is intended, in conjunction with the use of spacing and italics in the text, to help the reader to follow the main thread of Lucretius' argument. It is not presented as a complete summary of his teaching or a precise analysis of the structure of the poem.

It will be noticed that the first three books form, with a few digressions, a continuous chain of reasoning, leading up to the elaborate demonstration (III 417–829) that men are mortal. In the later Books the connecting thread is less definite. Here the poet is mainly concerned to show how various phenomena that appear to conflict with the materialistic principles laid down in Books I–III can in fact be explained in terms of those principles.

The digressions (including the introductions and conclusions of the several Books), apart from their immediate relevance to their context, serve a double purpose. They relieve the strain of following a long argument. And they illustrate, in one aspect or another, the blessings that flow from acceptance of the Epicurean faith.

No titles are assigned in the original to the separate Books.

*

Book I

MATTER AND SPACE

INTRODUCTION

Prayer to the creative force of Nature (personified as Venus) to inspire the poet, to bless his patron Memmius and to bring peace to the world (1–49).

Exhortation to Memmius to listen to an exposition of 'true reason' (50–61).

Praise of Epicurus for delivering mankind from superstition (62–79).

Superstition, its cause and cure (80–145).

SIX PRIMARY PROPOSITIONS

(i) Nothing is ever created out of nothing (146–214).
(ii) Nothing is ever annihilated (215–64).
(iii) Matter exists in the form of invisible particles (atoms) (265–328).
(iv) Besides matter, the universe contains empty space (vacuity) (329–417).
(v) The universe consists of matter (with its properties and accidents) and of vacuity and of nothing else (418–82).
(vi) The atoms are indestructible (483–634).

REFUTATION OF FALSE THEORIES

(a) The theory that everything consists of fire (Heraclitus) or some other single element (635–704).
(b) The theory that everything consists of two elements or of four (Empedocles) (705–829).
(c) The theory that the component parts of everything are of the same nature as the thing itself (Anaxagoras) (830–920).

TWO FURTHER PROPOSITIONS

(vii) The universe is boundless (921–1051).
(viii) The universe has no centre (1052–1113).

A WORD OF ENCOURAGEMENT

One discovery leads to another (1114–17).

Book II

MOVEMENTS AND SHAPES OF ATOMS

INTRODUCTION

The philosopher surveys struggling humanity from a citadel (1–61).

SIX PROPOSITIONS ON ATOMIC MOVEMENT

(i) The atoms are always on the move, either falling or rebounding (62–141).
(ii) They move faster than light (142–66).
  Digression: the world not made by gods (167–83).
(iii) The atoms normally move downwards (184–215).
(iv) Occasionally they swerve slightly from the vertical (216–93).
(v) They were never either more or less congested than now (294–307).
(vi) The apparent immobility of matter is an optical illusion (308–32).

SIX PROPOSITIONS ON ATOMIC SHAPE

(i) The various properties of objects are due to varieties in the size and shape of atoms (333–477).

(ii) The number of atomic shapes is large but finite (478–521).

(iii) The number of atoms of any one shape is infinite (522–68).
   Digression: creation balances destruction (569–81).

(iv) All visible objects are compounds of different kinds of atoms; with a *Digression* (589–660) on the worship of Mother Earth (582–699).

(v) Only certain compounds can exist (700–29).

(vi) The atoms themselves are devoid of colour (730–841), heat, sound, taste, and smell (842–64), and sentience (865–990); only so can we explain the ever-shifting panorama of nature (991–1022).

THREE GENERAL COROLLARIES

(i) Our world is one of an infinite number (1023–89).

(ii) Nature is self-regulating, without interference from the gods (1090–1104).

(iii) The world had a beginning and will soon have an end (1105–74).

Book III

LIFE AND MIND

INTRODUCTION

Praise of Epicurus for revealing the true nature of the universe (1–30).
The fear of death, and of something after death, is the root of evil (31–93).

SEVEN PROPOSITIONS

(i) The mind is a part of the body, not a harmony of the whole; so is the vital spirit (94–135).

(ii) The mind (lodged in the breast) and the spirit (diffused through the body) compose a single corporeal substance (136–76).

(iii) This substance is a compound of wind, air, heat and a very mobile fourth element, combined in varying proportions (177–322).

(iv) Life depends on the union of mind-spirit with body (323–69).

(v) The quantity of mind-spirit in the body is comparatively small (370–95).

(vi) Mind controls spirit (396–416).

(vii) Mind and spirit were born and will die (417–829).

Book VI

METEOROLOGY AND GEOLOGY

INTRODUCTION

Praise of Epicurus, the crowning glory of Athens (1–42).
Knowledge of natural phenomena helps to banish superstition (43–95).

CELESTIAL PHENOMENA

(i) Thunder (96–159), lightning (160–218), and thunderbolts (219–422).
(ii) Waterspouts (423–50), clouds (451–94), rain, etc. (495–534).

TERRESTRIAL PHENOMENA

(i) Earthquakes (535–607).
(ii) Why the sea is always the same size (608–38).
(iii) Volcanoes (639–702).
    Digression: difficulty of assigning the true cause to all phenomena (703–11).
(iv) Nile floods (712–37).
(v) Why some places are fatal to birds (738–847).
(vi) Peculiar properties of springs (848–905).
(vii) Magnets (906–1089).
(viii) Epidemics (1090–1286).

Book I

MATTER AND SPACE

*

MOTHER OF AENEAS and his race, delight of men and gods, life-giving Venus, it is your doing that under the wheeling constellations of the sky all nature teems with life, both the sea that buoys up our ships and the earth that yields our food. Through you all living creatures are conceived and come forth to look upon the sunlight. Before you the winds flee, and at your coming the clouds forsake the sky. For you the inventive earth flings up sweet flowers. For you the ocean levels laugh, the sky is calmed and glows with diffused radiance. When first the day puts on the aspect of spring, when in all its force the fertilizing breath of Zephyr is unleashed, then, great goddess, the birds of air give the first intimation of your entry; for yours is the power that has pierced them to the heart. Next the cattle run wild, frisk through the lush pastures and swim the swift-flowing streams. Spell-bound by your charm, they follow your lead with fierce desire. So throughout seas and uplands, rushing torrents, verdurous meadows and the leafy shelters of the birds, into the breasts of one and all you instil alluring love, so that with passionate longing they reproduce their several breeds.

Since you alone are the guiding power of the universe and without you nothing emerges into the shining sunlit world to grow in joy and loveliness, yours is the partnership I seek in striving to compose these lines *On the Nature of the*

Universe for my noble Memmius. For him, great goddess, you have willed outstanding excellence in every field and everlasting fame. For his sake, therefore, endow my verse with everlasting charm.

Meanwhile, grant that this brutal business of war by sea and land may everywhere be lulled to rest. For you alone have power to bestow on mortals the blessing of quiet peace. In your bosom Mars himself, supreme commander in this brutal business, flings himself down at times, laid low by the irremediable wound of love. Gazing upward, his neck a prostrate column, he fixes hungry eyes on you, great goddess, and gluts them with love. As he lies outstretched, his breath hangs upon your lips. Stoop, then, goddess most glorious, and enfold him at rest in your hallowed bosom and whisper with those lips sweet words of prayer, beseeching for the people of Rome untroubled peace. In this evil hour of my country's history, I cannot pursue my task with a mind at ease, as an illustrious scion of the house of Memmius cannot at such a crisis withhold his service from the common weal.

For what is to follow, my Memmius, lay aside your cares and lend undistracted ears and an attentive mind to true reason. Do not scornfully reject, before you have understood them, the gifts I have marshalled for you with zealous devotion. I will set out to discourse to you on the ultimate realities of heaven and the gods. I will reveal those *atoms* from which nature creates all things and increases and feeds them and into which, when they perish, nature again resolves them. To these in my discourse I commonly give such names as the 'raw material', or 'generative bodies' or 'seeds' of things. Or I may call them 'primary particles', because they come first and everything else is composed of them.

When human life lay grovelling in all men's sight, crushed to the earth under the dead weight of superstition whose grim features loured menacingly upon mortals from the four quarters of the sky, a man of Greece was first to raise mortal eyes in defiance, first to stand erect and brave the challenge. Fables of the gods did not crush him, nor the lightning flash and the growling menace of the sky. Rather, they quickened his manhood, so that he, first of all men, longed to smash the constraining locks of nature's doors. The vital vigour of his mind prevailed. He ventured far out beyond the flaming ramparts of the world and voyaged in mind throughout infinity. Returning victorious, he proclaimed to us what can be and what cannot: how a limit is fixed to the power of everything and an immovable frontier post. Therefore superstition in its turn lies crushed beneath his feet, and we by his triumph are lifted level with the skies.

One thing that worries me is the fear that you may fancy yourself embarking on an impious course, setting your feet on the path of sin. Far from it. More often it is this very superstition that is the mother of sinful and impious deeds. Remember how at Aulis the altar of the Virgin Goddess was foully stained with the blood of Iphigeneia by the leaders of the Greeks, the patterns of chivalry. The headband was bound about her virgin tresses and hung down evenly over both her cheeks. Suddenly she caught sight of her father standing sadly in front of the altar, the attendants beside him hiding the knife and her people bursting into tears when they saw her. Struck dumb with terror, she sank on her knees to the ground. Poor girl, at such a moment it did not

help her that she had been first to give the name of father
to a king. Raised by the hands of men, she was led trembling
to the altar. Not for her the sacrament of marriage and the
loud chant of Hymen. It was her fate in the very hour of
marriage to fall a sinless victim to a sinful rite, slaughtered
to her greater grief by a father's hand, so that a fleet might
sail under happy auspices. Such are the heights of wicked-
ness to which men are driven by superstition.

You yourself, if you surrender your judgment at any time
to the blood-curdling declamations of the prophets, will
want to desert our ranks. Only think what phantoms they
can conjure up to overturn the tenor of your life and wreck
your happiness with fear. And not without cause. For, if
men saw that a term was set to their troubles, they would
find strength in some way to withstand the hocus-pocus and
intimidations of the prophets. As it is, they have no power
of resistance, because they are haunted by the fear of eternal
punishment after death. They know nothing of the nature
of the spirit. Is it born, or is it implanted in us at birth?
Does it perish with us, dissolved by death, or does it visit
the murky depths and dreary sloughs of Hades? Or is it
transplanted by divine power into other creatures, as
described in the poems of our own Ennius, who first
gathered on the delectable slopes of Helicon an evergreen
garland destined to win renown among the nations of Italy?
Ennius indeed in his immortal verses proclaims that there
is also a Hell, which is peopled not by our actual spirits or
bodies but only by shadowy images, ghastly pale. It is from
this realm that he pictures the ghost of Homer, of unfading
memory, as appearing to him, shedding salt tears and revealing the nature of the universe.

I must therefore give an account of celestial phenomena,
explaining the movements of sun and moon and also the

forces that determine events on earth. Next, and no less important, we must look with keen insight into the make-up of spirit and mind: we must consider those alarming phantasms that strike upon our minds when they are awake but disordered by sickness, or when they are buried in slumber, so that we seem to see and hear before us men whose dead bones lie in the embraces of earth.

I am well aware that it is not easy to elucidate in Latin verse the obscure discoveries of the Greeks. The poverty of our language and the novelty of the theme compel me often to coin new words for the purpose. But your merit and the joy I hope to derive from our delightful friendship encourage me to face any task however hard. This it is that leads me to stay awake through the quiet of the night, studying how by choice of words and the poet's art I can display before your mind a clear light by which you can gaze into the heart of hidden things.

This dread and darkness of the mind cannot be dispelled by the sunbeams, the shining shafts of day, but only by an understanding of the outward form and inner workings of nature. In tackling this theme, our starting-point will be this principle: *Nothing can ever be created by divine power out of nothing.* The reason why all mortals are so gripped by fear is that they see all sorts of things happening on the earth and in the sky with no discernible cause, and these they attribute to the will of a god. Accordingly, when we have seen that nothing can be created out of nothing, we shall then have a clearer picture of the path ahead, the problem of how things are created and occasioned without the aid of the gods.

First then, if things were made out of nothing, any species could spring from any source and nothing would require seed. Men could arise from the sea and scaly fish from the earth, and birds could be hatched out of the sky. Cattle and other domestic animals and every kind of wild beast, multiplying indiscriminately, would occupy cultivated and waste lands alike. The same fruits would not grow constantly on the same trees, but they would keep changing: any tree might bear any fruit. If each species were not composed of its own generative bodies, why should each be born always of the same kind of mother? Actually, since each is formed out of specific seeds, it is born and emerges into the sunlit world only from a place where there exists the right material, the right kind of atoms. This is why everything cannot be born of everything, but a specific power of generation inheres in specific objects.

Again, why do we see roses appear in spring, grain in summer's heat, grapes under the spell of autumn? Surely, because it is only after specific seeds have drifted together at their own proper time that every created thing stands revealed, when the season is favourable and the life-giving earth can safely deliver delicate growths into the sunlit world. If they were made out of nothing, they would spring up suddenly after varying lapses of time and at abnormal seasons, since there would of course be no primary bodies which could be prevented by the harshness of the season from entering into generative unions. Similarly, in order that things might grow, there would be no need of any lapse of time for the accumulation of seed. Tiny tots would turn suddenly into grown men, and trees would shoot up spontaneously out of the earth. But it is obvious that none of these things happens, since everything grows gradually, as is natural, from a specific seed and retains its specific character. It is a fair inference that each is increased and nourished by its own raw material.

Here is a further point. Without seasonable showers the

earth cannot send up gladdening growths. Lacking food, animals cannot reproduce their kind or sustain life. This points to the conclusion that many elements are common to many things, as letters are to words, rather than to the theory that anything can come into existence without atoms.

Or again, why has not nature been able to produce men on such a scale that they could ford the ocean on foot or demolish high mountains with their hands or prolong their lives over many generations? Surely, because each thing requires for its birth a particular material which determines what can be produced. It must therefore be admitted that nothing can be made out of nothing, because everything must be generated from a seed before it can emerge into the unresisting air.

Lastly, we see that tilled plots are superior to untilled, and their fruits are improved by cultivation. This is because the earth contains certain atoms which we rouse to productivity by turning the fruitful clods with the ploughshare and stirring up the soil. But for these, you would see great improvements arising spontaneously without any aid from our labours.

The second great principle is this: *nature resolves everything into its component atoms and never reduces anything to nothing.* If anything were perishable in all its parts, anything might perish all of a sudden and vanish from sight. There would be no need of any force to separate its parts and loosen their links. In actual fact, since everything is composed of indestructible seeds, nature obviously does not allow anything to perish till it has encountered a force that shatters it with a blow or creeps into chinks and unknits it.

If the things that are banished from the scene by age are annihilated through the exhaustion of their material, from what source does Venus bring back the several races of animals into the light of life? And, when they are brought back, where does the inventive earth find for each the special food required for its sustenance and growth? From what fount is the sea replenished by its native springs and the streams that flow into it from afar? Whence does the ether draw nutriment for the stars? For everything consisting of a mortal body must have been exhausted by the long day of time, the illimitable past. If throughout this bygone eternity there have persisted bodies from which the universe has been perpetually renewed, they must certainly be possessed of immortality. Therefore things cannot be reduced to nothing.

Again, all objects would regularly be destroyed by the same force and the same cause, were it not that they are sustained by imperishable matter more or less tightly fastened together. Why, a mere touch would be enough to bring about destruction supposing there were no imperishable bodies whose union could be dissolved only by the appropriate force. Actually, because the fastenings of the atoms are of various kinds while their matter is imperishable, compound objects remain intact until one of them encounters a force that proves strong enough to break up its particular constitution. Therefore nothing returns to nothing, but everything is resolved into its constituent bodies.

Lastly, showers perish when father ether has flung them down into the lap of mother earth. But the crops spring up fresh and gay; the branches on the trees burst into leaf; the trees themselves grow and are weighed down with fruit. Hence in turn man and brute draw nourishment. Hence we see flourishing cities blest with children and every leafy thicket loud with new broods of songsters. Hence in lush pastures cattle wearied by their bulk fling down their bodies, and the white milky juice oozes from their swollen udders. Hence a new generation frolic friskily on wobbly legs through the fresh grass, their young minds tipsy with undiluted milk. Visible objects therefore do not perish utterly, since nature repairs one thing from another and allows nothing to be born without the aid of another's death.

Well, Memmius, I have taught you that things cannot be created out of nothing nor, once born, be summoned back to nothing. Perhaps, however, you are becoming mistrustful of my words, because these atoms of mine are not visible to the eye. Consider, therefore, this further evidence of *bodies whose existence you must acknowledge though they cannot be seen.* First, wind, when its force is roused, whips up waves, founders tall ships and scatters cloud-rack. Sometimes scouring plains with hurricane force it strews them with huge trees and batters mountain peaks with blasts that hew down forests. Such is wind in its fury, when it whoops aloud with a mad menace in its shouting. Without question, therefore, there must be invisible particles of wind which sweep sea and land and the clouds in the sky, swooping upon them and whirling them along in a headlong hurricane. In the way they flow and the havoc they spread they are no different from a torrential flood of water when it rushes down in a sudden spate from the mountain heights, swollen by heavy rains, and heaps together wreckage from the forest and entire trees. Soft though it is by nature, the sudden shock of oncoming water is more than even stout bridges can withstand, so furious is the force with which the turbid, storm-flushed torrent surges against their piers. With a mighty roar it lays them low, rolling huge rocks under its waves and brushing aside every obstacle from its course. Such, therefore, must be the movement of blasts of wind also. When they have come surging along some course like a rushing river, they push obstacles before them and buffet them with repeated blows; and sometimes, eddying round and round, they snatch them up and carry them along in a swiftly circling vortex. Here then is proof upon proof that winds have invisible bodies, since in their actions and behaviour they are found to rival great rivers, whose bodies are plain to see.

Then again, we smell the various scents of things though we never see them approaching our nostrils. Similarly, heat and cold cannot be detected by our eyes, and we do not see sounds. Yet all these must be composed of bodies, since they are able to impinge upon our senses. For nothing can touch or be touched except body.

Again, clothes hung out on a surf-beaten shore grow moist. Spread in the sun they grow dry. But we do not see how the moisture has soaked into them, nor again how it has been dispelled by the heat. It follows that the moisture is split up into minute parts which the eye cannot possibly see.

Again, in the course of many annual revolutions of the sun a ring is worn thin next to the finger with continual rubbing. Dripping water hollows a stone. A curved ploughshare, iron though it is, dwindles imperceptibly in the furrow. We see the cobble-stones of the highway worn by the feet of many wayfarers. The bronze statues by the city gates show their right hands worn thin by the touch of travellers who have greeted them in passing. We see that all these are being diminished, since they are worn away. But to perceive what particles drop off at any particular time is a power grudged to us by our ungenerous sense of sight.

To sum up, whatever is added to things gradually by nature and the passage of days, causing a cumulative increase, eludes the most attentive scrutiny of our eyes. Conversely, you cannot see what objects lose by the wastage of age – sheer sea-cliffs, for instance, exposed to prolonged erosion by the mordant brine – or at what time the loss occurs. It follows that nature works through the agency of invisible bodies.

On the other hand, things are not hemmed in by the pressure of solid bodies in a tight mass. This is because *there is vacuity in things*. A grasp of this fact will be helpful to you in many respects and will save you from much bewildered doubting and questioning about the universe and from mistrust of my teaching. Well then, by vacuity I mean intangible and empty space. If it did not exist, things could not move at all. For the distinctive action of matter, which is counteraction and obstruction, would be in force always and everywhere. Nothing could proceed, because nothing would give it a starting-point by receding. As it is, we see with our own eyes at sea and on land and high up in the sky that all sorts of things in all sorts of ways are on the move. If there were no empty space, these things would be denied the power of restless movement – or rather, they could not possibly have come into existence, embedded as they would have been in motionless matter.

Besides, there are clear indications that things that pass for solid are in fact porous. Even in rocks a trickle of water seeps through into caves, and copious drops ooze from every surface. Food percolates to every part of an animal's body. Trees grow and bring forth their fruit in season, because their food is distributed throughout their length from the tips of the roots through the trunk and along every branch. Noises pass through walls and fly into closed buildings. Freezing cold penetrates to the bones. If there were no vacancies through which the various bodies could make their way, none of these phenomena would be possible.

Again, why do we find some things outweigh others of equal volume? If there is as much matter in a ball of wool as in one of lead, it is natural that it should weigh as heavily, since it is the function of matter to press everything downwards, while it is the function of space on the other hand to remain weightless. Accordingly, when one thing is not less bulky than another but obviously lighter, it plainly declares that there is more vacuum in it, while the heavier object proclaims that there is more matter in it and much less empty space. We have therefore reached the goal of our diligent enquiry: there is in things an admixture of what we call vacuity.

In case you should be misled on this question by the idle imagining of certain theorists, I must anticipate their argument. They maintain that water yields and opens a penetrable path to the scaly bodies of fish that push against it, because they leave spaces behind them into which the yielding water can flow together. In the same way, they suppose, other things can move by mutually changing places, although every place remains filled. This theory has been adopted utterly without warrant. For how can the fish advance till the water has given way? And how can the water retire when the fish cannot move? There are thus only two alternatives: either all bodies are devoid of movement, or you must admit that things contain an admixture of vacuity whereby each is enabled to make the first move.

Lastly, if two bodies suddenly spring apart from contact on a broad surface, all the intervening space must be void until it is occupied by air. However quickly the air rushes in all round, the entire space cannot be filled instanta-

neously. The air must occupy one spot after another until it
has taken possession of the whole space. If anyone supposes
that this consequence of such springing apart is made
possible by the condensation of air, he is mistaken. For
condensation implies that something that was full becomes
empty, or *vice versâ*. And I contend that air could not
condense so as to produce this effect; or at any rate, if there
were no vacuum, it could not thus shrink into itself and
draw its parts together.

However many pleas you may advance to prolong the argument, you must end by admitting that there is vacuity in
things. There are many other proofs I could add to the pile
in order to strengthen conviction; but for an acute intelligence these small clues should suffice to enable you to
discover the rest for yourself. As hounds that range the hills
often smell out the lairs of wild beasts screened in thickets,
when once they have got on to the right trail, so in such
questions one thing will lead on to another, till you can
succeed by yourself in tracking down the truth to its lurking-
places and dragging it forth. If you grow weary and relax
from the chase, there is one thing, Memmius, that I can
safely promise you: my honeyed tongue will pour from the
treasury of my breast such generous draughts, drawn from
inexhaustible springs, that I am afraid slow-plodding age
may creep through my limbs and unbolt the bars of my life
before the full flood of my arguments on any single point
has flowed in verse through your ears.

To pick up the thread of my discourse, all nature as it is in
itself consists of two things – bodies and the vacant space in
which the bodies are situated and through which they move
in different directions. The existence of bodies is vouched
for by the agreement of the senses. If a belief resting directly

on this foundation is not valid, there will be no standard to
which we can refer any doubt on obscure questions for
rational confirmation. If there were no place and space,
which we call vacuity, these bodies could not be situated
anywhere or move in any direction whatever. This I have
just demonstrated. It remains to show that *nothing exists that
is distinct both from body and from vacuity* and could be ranked
with the others as a third substance. For whatever *is* must
also be something. If it offers resistance to touch, however
light and slight, it will increase the mass of body by such
amount, great or small, as it may amount to, and will rank
with it. If, on the other hand, it is intangible, so that it
offers no resistance whatever to anything passing through
it, then it will be that empty space which we call vacuity.
Besides, whatever it may be in itself, either it will act in
some way, or react to other things acting upon it, or else
it will be such that things can be and happen in it. But
without body nothing can act or react; and nothing can
afford a place except emptiness and vacancy. Therefore,
besides matter and vacuity, we cannot include in the
number of things any third substance that can either affect our
senses at any time or be grasped by the reasoning of our minds.

You will find that anything that can be named is either a
property or an accident of these two. A *property* is something
that cannot be detached or separated from a thing without
destroying it, as weight is a property of rocks, heat of fire,
fluidity of water, tangibility of all bodies, intangibility of
vacuum. On the other hand, servitude and liberty, poverty
and riches, war and peace, and all other things whose
advent or departure leaves the essence of a thing intact, all
these it is our practice to call by their appropriate name,
accidents.

Similarly, time by itself does not exist; but from things

themselves there results a sense of what has already taken place, what is now going on and what is to ensue. It must not be claimed that anyone can sense time by itself apart from the movement of things or their restful immobility.

Again, when men say it *is* a fact that Helen was ravished or the Trojans were conquered, do not let anyone drive you to the admission that any such event *is* independently of any object, on the ground that the generations of men of whom these events were accidents have been swept away by the irrevocable lapse of time. For we could put it that whatever has taken place is an accident of a particular tract of earth or of the space it occupied. If there had been no matter and no space or place in which things could happen, no spark of love kindled by the beauty of Tyndareus' daughter would ever have stolen into the breast of Phrygian Paris to light that dazzling blaze of pitiless war; no Wooden Horse, unmarked by the sons of Troy, would have set the towers of Ilium aflame through the midnight issue of Greeks from its womb. So you may see that events cannot be said to *be* by themselves like matter or in the same sense as space. Rather, you should describe them as accidents of matter, or of the place in which things happen.

Material objects are of two kinds, atoms and compounds of atoms. The atoms themselves cannot be swamped by any force, for they are preserved indefinitely by their absolute solidity. Admittedly, it is hard to believe that anything can exist that is absolutely solid. The lightning stroke from the sky penetrates closed buildings, as do shouts and other noises. Iron glows molten in the fire, and hot rocks are cracked by untempered scorching. Hard gold is softened and melted by heat; and bronze, ice-like, is liquefied by flame. Both heat and piercing cold seep through silver, since we feel both alike when a cooling shower of water is poured into a goblet that we hold ceremonially in our hands. All these facts point to the conclusion that nothing is really solid. But sound reasoning and nature itself drive us to the opposite conclusion. Pay attention, therefore, while I demonstrate in a few lines that there exist certain bodies that are absolutely solid and indestructible, namely those atoms which according to our teaching are the seeds or prime units of things from which the whole universe is built up.

In the first place, we have found that nature is twofold, consisting of two totally different things, matter and the space in which things happen. Hence each of these must exist by itself without admixture of the other. For, where there is empty space (what we call vacuity), there matter is not; where matter exists, there cannot be a vacuum. Therefore the prime units of matter are solid and free from vacuity.

Again, since composite things contain some vacuum, the surrounding matter must be solid. For you cannot reasonably maintain that anything can hide vacuity and hold it within its body unless you allow that the container itself is solid. And what contains the vacuum in things can only be an accumulation of matter. Hence matter, which possesses absolute solidity, can be everlasting when other things are decomposed.

Again, if there were no empty space, everything would be one solid mass; if there were no material objects with the property of filling the space they occupy, all existing space would be utterly void. It is clear, then, that there is an alternation of matter and vacuity, mutually distinct, since the whole is neither completely full nor completely empty. There are therefore solid bodies, causing the distinction between empty space and full. And these, as I have just shown, can be neither decomposed by blows from without nor invaded and unknit from within nor destroyed by any other form of assault. For it seems that a thing without vacuum can be neither knocked to bits nor snapped nor chopped in two by cutting; nor can it let in moisture or seeping cold or piercing fire, the universal agents of destruction. The more vacuum a thing contains within it, the more readily it yields to these assailants. Hence, if the units of matter are solid and without vacuity, as I have shown, they must be everlasting.

Yet again, if the matter in things had not been everlasting, everything by now would have gone back to nothing, and the things we see would be the product of rebirth out of nothing. But, since I have already shown that nothing can be created out of nothing nor any existing thing be summoned back to nothing, the atoms must be made of imperishable stuff into which everything can be resolved in the end, so that there may be a stock of matter for building the world anew. The atoms, therefore, are absolutely solid and unalloyed. In no other way could they have survived throughout infinite time to keep the world in being.

Furthermore, if nature had set no limit to the breaking of things, the particles of matter in the course of ages would have been ground so small that nothing could be generated from them so as to attain in the fullness of time to the summit of its growth. For we see that anything can be more speedily disintegrated than put together again. Hence, what the long day of time, the bygone eternity, has already shaken and loosened to fragments could never in the residue of time be reconstructed. As it is, there is evidently a limit set to breaking, since we see that everything is renewed and each according to its kind has a fixed period in which to grow to its prime.

Here is a further argument. Granted that the particles of matter are absolutely solid, we can still explain the composition and behaviour of soft things – air, water, earth, fire – by their intermixture with empty space. On the other hand, supposing the atoms to be soft, we cannot account for the origin of hard flint and iron. For there would be no foundation for nature to build on. Therefore there must be bodies strong in their unalloyed solidity by whose closer clustering things can be knit together and display unyielding toughness.

If we suppose that there is no limit set to the breaking of matter, we must still admit that material objects consist of particles which throughout eternity have resisted the forces of destruction. To say that these are breakable does not square with the fact that they have survived throughout eternity under a perpetual bombardment of innumerable blows.

Again, there is laid down for each thing a specific limit to its growth and its tenure of life, and the laws of nature ordain what each can do and what it cannot. No species is ever changed, but each remains so much itself that every kind of bird displays on its body its own specific markings. This is a further proof that their bodies are composed of changeless matter. For, if the atoms could yield in any way to change, there would be no certainty as to what could arise and what could not, at what point the power of everything was limited by an immovable frontier-post; nor could successive generations so regularly repeat the nature, behaviour, habits and movements of their parents.

To proceed with our argument, there is an ultimate point in visible objects which represents the smallest thing that can be seen. So also there must be an ultimate point in objects that lie below the limit of perception by our senses. This point is without parts and is the smallest thing that can exist. It never has been and never will be able to exist by itself, but only as one primary part of something else. It is with a mass of such parts, solidly jammed together in order, that matter is filled up. Since they cannot exist by themselves, they must needs stick together in a mass from which they cannot by any means be prized loose. The atoms therefore are absolutely solid and unalloyed, consisting of a mass of least parts tightly packed together. They are not compounds formed by the coalescence of their parts, but bodies of absolute and everlasting solidity. To these nature allows no loss or diminution, but guards them as seeds for things. If there are no such least parts, even the smallest bodies will consist of an infinite number of parts, since they can always be halved and their halves halved again without limit. On this showing, what difference will there be between the whole universe and the very least of things? None at all. For, however endlessly infinite the universe may be, yet the smallest things will equally consist of an infinite number of parts. Since true reason cries out against this and denies that the mind can believe it, you must needs give in and admit that there are least parts which themselves are partless. Granted that these parts exist, you must needs admit that the atoms they compose are also solid and everlasting. But, if all things were compelled by all-creating nature to be broken up into these least parts, nature would lack the power to rebuild anything out of them. For partless objects cannot have the essential properties of generative matter — those varieties of attachment, weight, impetus, impact and movement on which everything depends.

For all these reasons, *those who have imagined that the raw material of things is fire and the universe consists of fire alone have evidently wandered far from the truth.* Of these the first cham-

pion to plunge into the fray was Heraclitus, illustrious for
the darkness of his speech, though rather among the lighter-
witted of the Greeks than among those who are earnest
seekers after truth. For fools are more impressed and
intrigued by what they detect under a screen of riddling
words, and accept as true what pleasantly tickles their ears
with a jingle of meretricious melody. I should like to know
how things can be so manifold if they are created out of
nothing but sheer fire. It would not help if hot fire were
condensed or rarefied, so long as the particles of fire retained
the same nature that fire possesses as a whole. Its heat would
simply be fiercer as its parts were more concentrated,
milder as they were dispersed and dissipated. There is no
further effect that you could attribute to such causes – no
possibility that the immense variety of things could result
from variations in the density or rarity of fire. Even these
variations in density could not occur unless we allow in
things an intermixture of vacuity. But, because these
theorists see many things run counter to their theories, they
dodge the issue and decline to leave any pure vacuum in
things. Shunning the steep, they lose the true path. They
do not see that without vacuity everything would be condensed and would become one body which could not throw
off anything at high speed from itself, as blazing fire throws
off light and heat, so that you can see that its parts are not
solidly compacted.

If, on the other hand, they think that there is some other
way in which fires in combination can be quenched and
change their substance, then obviously – if they do not
shrink from any implication of this view – the fieriness must
be completely annihilated and whatever emerges must be a
new creation out of nothing. For, if ever anything is so
transformed as to overstep its own limits, this means the

immediate death of what was before. It follows that they
must leave something intact, or you would find everything
reduced to nothing and the stock of things reborn and
reinvigorated from nothing. As it is, there are certain
definite bodies that always keep the same nature, and it is
by the withdrawal or advent of these and their reshuffling
that things change their nature and material objects are
transformed. And these primary bodies cannot be fiery. So
long as they possessed and retained a fiery nature, it would
make no odds if some of them were detached and withdrawn and others tacked on and some were reshuffled.
Whatever they created would still be simply fire. The truth,
as I maintain, is this: there are certain bodies whose
impacts, movements, order, position and shapes produce
fires. When their order is changed, they change their
nature. In themselves they do not resemble fire or anything
else that can bombard our senses with particles or impinge
on our organs of touch.

To say, as Heraclitus does, that everything is fire, and
nothing can be numbered among things as a reality except
fire, seems utterly crazy. On the basis of the senses he
attacks and unsettles the senses – the foundation of all belief
and the only source of his knowledge of that which he calls
fire. He believes that the senses clearly perceive fire, but
not the other things that are in fact no less clear. This strikes
me as not only pointless but mad. For what is to be our
standard of reference? What can be a surer guide to the
distinction of true from false than our own senses? What
grounds have we for taking away everything else and leaving
fire, any more than for taking away fire and leaving some
other thing? Either procedure appears equally insane.

For this reason those who have thought that fire is the raw
material of things and the universe can consist of fire, and

those who have made *air* the starting-point for the growth
of things or have supposed that *water* by itself could form
everything or that *earth* could create all things and be
transformed into their natures – all these have evidently
wandered far from the truth.

Not less mistaken are those who make the elements two-fold, coup-
ling air with fire and earth with water, *and those who think
that everything can grow from four elements*, fire and earth and
wind and rain. Conspicuous among these is Empedocles of
Acragas, born in the three-cornered confines of that Isle
round which surges the Ionian deep, rushing far into creeks
and dashing up salt spray from its grey-green billows. The
sea that parts it from Italian shores runs headlong through
its narrow channel. Here is deadly Charybdis. Here the
rumbling of Etna's flames is a warning that they are rallying
their wrath till the mountain has gathered strength to dis-
gorge unprisoned fire once again from its throat and fling
back against the sky the lightning of its flame. This great
country is acknowledged to have many claims to the admira-
tion of mankind and the attention of sight-seers. But, for all
its wealth of good things and its ample garrison of men, it
has surely held nothing more glorious than this man, nothing
holier, nothing more wonderful, nothing more precious.
Indeed, the songs that took shape in his divine breast proclaim in ringing tones such glorious discoveries that he
scarcely seems a scion of mortal stock. Empedocles and
those lesser men of whom we have spoken above, who rank
far and away below him, have certainly made many excellent
and divine discoveries and uttered oracles from the inner
sanctuary of their hearts with more sanctity and far surer
reason than those the Delphic prophetess pronounces,
drugged by the laurel fumes from Apollo's tripod. Yet

among the very foundations of things they have come to grief. Great as they were, great has been their fall.

Their first error is this: they postulate movement while banishing empty space from the universe, and they admit the existence of soft and flimsy things – air, sun, fire, soils, animals, vegetables – without allowing their bodies an intermixture of vacuity.

Secondly, they acknowledge no limit to the splitting of things, no rest from crumbling, no prime unit of matter, although we see that every object has an ultimate point that seems to our senses to be the smallest, from which you may infer that the things you cannot perceive have also an ultimate point which actually is the smallest. Besides, since they rank as elements soft things which we perceive to be neither birthless nor deathless, the universe ought by now to have returned to nothing and whatever exists ought to be a new creation and growth out of nothing, both of which suppositions you already know to be false. Furthermore, these supposed elements are in many ways hurtful and lethal to one another, so that they will either be destroyed on contact or will rush apart, as we see lightning flashes, rain-clouds and winds rush apart when they have been driven together by a storm.

Again, if everything is created from four things and resolved into them, why should we say that these are the elements of things rather than the reverse – that other things are the elements of these? For one gives birth to another continually, and they interchange their colours and their entire natures throughout the whole of time. If, on the other hand, you believe that particles of fire and earth, airy wind and watery moisture, combine without changing their natures in combination, then nothing can be created from them, either animate or (like a tree) with inanimate body.

PRAIRIE STATE COLLEGE
LEARNING CENTER

3 2783 00021 0107

For each element in a composite assemblage will betray its
own nature; air will appear mixed with earth, and fire will
remain side by side with moisture. But in fact the elements,
in giving birth to things, must contribute a nature that is
hidden and viewless, so that nothing may show that conflicts
with the thing created and prevents it from being
distinctively itself.

These authors trace everything back to the sky and its
fires. First they make fire transform itself into the winds of
air; hence is born rain, and from rain is created earth. Then
the process is reversed: first from earth is born moisture,
then comes air, then fire. And things never cease to interchange, migrating from heaven to earth, from earth to the
starry firmament. This is something elements ought never
to do. For it is essential that something should remain
immutable, or everything would be reduced to nothing.
For, if ever anything is so transformed that it oversteps its
own limits, this means the immediate death of what was
before. Therefore, since the substances just mentioned
enter into interchange, they must needs consist of other
substances that cannot be altered, so that you may not find
everything reduced to nothing. You ought rather to postulate bodies possessed of such a nature that, if they happen to
have created fire, they only need a few subtractions and
additions and some change of order and movement to make
gusty air. In this way we can account for any change from
one thing to another.

'But,' you say, 'observation clearly shows that all growing
things do grow up into the gusty air out of the earth and it
is from the earth that they draw their food. And, unless an
auspicious season gives free play to the rain, so that trees
reel beneath the dissolving cloud-rack, and unless the sun
in turn provides fostering warmth, there can be no growth

of crops, trees, or animals.' Yes, and unless we ourselves
were sustained by dry food and fluid juices, our bodies
would waste away till every bit of life had escaped from all
our sinews and bones. There can be no doubt that we are
fed and sustained by certain specific things, other things by
others, and so forth. Obviously, it is because there are in
things many elements common to many things commingled
in many ways that various things draw their food from
various sources. It often makes a big difference in what
combinations and positions the selfsame elements occur,
and what motions they mutually pass on or take over. For
the same elements compose sky, sea and lands, rivers and
sun, crops, trees and animals, but they are moving
differently and in different combinations. Consider how in
my verses, for instance, you see many letters common to
many words; yet you must admit that different verses and
words differ in substance and in audible sound. So much can
be accomplished by letters through mere change of order.
But the elements can bring more factors into play so as to
create things in all their variety.

Now let us look into the theory of Anaxagoras, which the
Greeks call *homoiomereia;* the poverty of our native tongue
will not let me translate the word, but the thing itself can
be expressed readily enough. Understand, then, that in
speaking of the *homoiomereia* of things Anaxagoras means that
bones are formed of minute miniature bones, flesh of
minute miniature morsels of flesh, blood by the coalescence
of many drops of blood; gold consists of grains of gold;
earth is a conglomeration of little earths, fire of fires,
moisture of moistures. And he pictures everything else as
formed in the same way. At the same time he does not
admit any vacuum in things, or any limit to the splitting of

matter, on both of which counts he seems to me guilty of the same error as the others. Add to this that he makes the elements too frail, if indeed we can allow the name of 'elements' to bodies that have the same nature as the things themselves, that suffer and decay no less than they do and are not shielded by any force from destruction. For which of these things will withstand violent assault, so as to escape extinction in the very jaws of death? Will fire or water or air? Will blood or bones survive? Nothing, I maintain, will escape, where everything is as perishable as those objects that we see vanishing from before our eyes under stress of some force or other. In proof of the impossibility of such annihilation and regrowth from nothing, I appeal to the evidence already adduced.

Again, since food builds up and nourishes our bodies, our veins and blood and bones and sinews must be composed of matter unlike themselves. Alternatively, if it is alleged that all foods are of mixed substance and contain little morsels of sinews and bones and veins and drops of blood, it must be supposed that all food, whether solid or fluid, consists of unlike matter, namely of a mixture of bones and sinews, pus and blood. Similarly, if the material of all the things that grow out of the earth occurs in the earth, earth must consist of unlike matter which rises out of it. Turn to other phenomena, and the same words will hold good. If flame, smoke and ashes lurk unseen in wood, then wood must consist of unlike matter which rises out of it.

Here there is left some scanty cover for escaping detection, and Anaxagoras avails himself of it. He asserts that there is in everything a mixture of everything, but all the ingredients escape detection except the one whose particles are most numerous and conspicuous and lie nearest the surface. This is far removed from the truth. Otherwise it would naturally happen that corn, when it is crushed by the dire force of the grindstone, would often show some sign of blood, and that blood would exude when we crush between stones any of those things that derive material from our bodies. Similarly, grass and water ought often to emit sweet drops of the same flavour as the milk in the udders of fleecy ewes. When clods of soil are crumpled, finely divided particles of different plants and grains and leaves ought to become visible, lurking among the soil. When sticks are snapped, ashes and smoke ought to be revealed, and tiny hidden fires. But observation plainly shows that none of these things happens. It is clear therefore that one sort of thing is not intermingled with another in this way, but there must be in things a mixture of invisible seeds that are common to many sorts.

'But,' you may object, 'it often happens in mountainous country that nearby tops of tall trees are rubbed together by the force of a gale till suddenly they blossom out into a blaze of flame.' Agreed. And yet there is no fire embedded in the wood. What it does contain is a multitude of seeds of heat. which start a conflagration in the forest only when they have been concentrated by rubbing. If there were ready-made flame concealed in the wood, the fires could not be hidden for any length of time; they would spread havoc through the woodland and burn the trees to ashes. Now do you see the point of my previous remark, that it makes a great difference in what combinations and positions the same elements occur and what motions they mutually pass on and take over, so that with a little reshuffling the same ones may produce forests and fires? This is just how the words themselves are formed, by a little reshuffling of the letters, when we pronounce 'forests' and 'fires' as two distinct utterances.

If you cannot account for what you see happen without inventing particles of matter with the same sort of nature as the whole objects, there is an end of your elements altogether: you will have to postulate particles that shake their sides with uproarious guffaws and bedew their cheeks with salt tears.

And now pay special attention to what follows and listen more intently. I am well aware how full it is of obscurity. But high hope of fame has struck my heart with its sharp goad and in so doing has implanted in my breast the sweet love of the Muses. That is the spur that lends my spirit strength to pioneer through pathless tracts of their Pierian realm where no foot has ever trod before. What joy it is to light upon virgin springs and drink their waters. What joy to pluck new flowers and gather for my brow a glorious garland from fields whose blossoms were never yet wreathed by the Muses round any head. This is my reward for teaching on these lofty topics, for struggling to loose men's minds from the tight knots of superstition and shedding on dark corners the bright beams of my song that irradiate everything with the sparkle of the Muses. My art is not without a purpose. Physicians, when they wish to treat children with a nasty dose of wormwood, first smear the rim of the cup with a sweet coat of yellow honey. The children, too young as yet for foresight, are lured by the sweetness at their lips into swallowing the bitter draught. So they are tricked but not trapped, for the treatment restores them to health. In the same way our doctrine often seems unpalatable to those who have not sampled it, and the multitude shrink from it. That is why I have tried to administer it to you in the dulcet strains of poesy, coated with the sweet honey of the Muses. My object has been to engage your mind with my verses while you gain insight into the nature of the universe and the pattern of its architecture.

Well then, since I have shown that there are completely solid indestructible particles of matter flying about through all eternity, let us elucidate whether or not there is any limit to their number. Similarly, as we have found that there is a vacuum, the place or space in which things happen, let us see whether its whole extent is limited or whether it stretches far and wide into immeasurable depths.

Learn, therefore, that *the universe is not bounded in any direction.* If it were, it would necessarily have a limit somewhere. But clearly a thing cannot have a limit unless there is something outside to limit it, so that the eye can follow it up to a certain point but not beyond. Since you must admit that there is nothing outside the universe, it can have no limit and is accordingly without end or measure. It makes no odds in which part of it you may take your stand: whatever spot anyone may occupy, the universe stretches away from him just the same in all directions without limit. Suppose for a moment that the whole of space were bounded and that someone made his way to its uttermost boundary and threw a flying dart. Do you choose to suppose that the missile, hurled with might and main, would speed along the course on which it was aimed? Or do you think something would block the way and stop it? You must assume one alternative or the other. But neither of them leaves you a loophole. Both force you to admit that the universe continues without end. Whether there is some obstacle lying on the boundary line that prevents the dart from going farther on its course or whether it flies on beyond, it cannot in fact have started from the boundary. With this argument I will pursue you. Wherever you may place the ultimate limit of things, I will ask you: 'Well then, what does happen to the dart?' The upshot is that the boundary cannot stand firm anywhere, and final escape from this conclusion is precluded by the limitless possibility of running away from it.

It is a matter of observation that one thing is limited by another. The hills are demarcated by air, and air by the hills. Land sets bounds to sea, and sea to every land. But the universe has nothing outside to limit it.

Further, if all the space in the universe were shut in and confined on every side by definite boundaries, the supply of matter would already have accumulated by its own weight at the bottom, and nothing could happen under the dome of the sky – indeed, there would be no sky and no sunlight, since all the available matter would have settled down and would be lying in a heap throughout eternity. As it is, no rest is given to the atoms, because there is no bottom where they can accumulate and take up their abode. Things go on happening all the time through ceaseless movement in every direction; and atoms of matter bouncing up from below are supplied out of the infinite. There is therefore a limitless abyss of space, such that even the dazzling flashes of the lightning cannot traverse it in their course, racing through an interminable tract of time, nor can they even shorten the distance still to be covered. So vast is the scope that lies open to things far and wide without limit in any dimension.

The universe is restrained from setting any limit to itself by nature, which compels body to be bounded by vacuum and vacuum by body. Thus nature either makes them both infinite in alternation, or else one of them, if it is not bounded by the other, must extend in a pure state without limit. Space, however, being infinite, so must matter be. Otherwise neither sea nor land nor the bright zones of the sky nor mortal beings nor the holy bodies of the gods could endure for one brief hour of time. The supply of matter would be shaken loose from combination and swept through the vastness of the void in isolated particles; or rather, it would never have coalesced to form anything, since its scattered particles could never have been driven into union.

Certainly the atoms did not post themselves purposefully in due order by an act of intelligence, nor did they stipulate what movements each should perform. As they have been rushing everlastingly throughout all space in their myriads, undergoing a myriad changes under the disturbing impact of collisions, they have experienced every variety of movement and conjunction till they have fallen into the particular pattern by which this world of ours is constituted. This world has persisted many a long year, having once been set going in the appropriate motions. From these everything else follows. The rivers replenish the thirsty sea with profuse streams of water. Incubated by the sun's heat, the earth renews its fruits, and the brood of animals that springs from it grows lustily. The gliding fires of ether sustain their life. None of these results would be possible if there were not an ample supply of matter to bounce up out of infinite space in replacement of all that is lost. Just as animals deprived of food waste away through loss of body, so everything must decay as soon as its supply of matter goes astray and is cut off.

Whatever world the atoms have combined to form, impacts from without cannot preserve it at every point. By continual battering they can hold back part of it till others come along to make good the deficiency. But they are compelled now and then to bounce back and in so doing to leave space and time for the atoms to break loose from combination. It is thus essential that there should be great numbers of atoms coming up. Indeed, the impacts them-

selves could not be maintained without an unlimited supply
of matter from all quarters.

There is one belief, Memmius, that you must beware of
entertaining – *the theory that everything tends towards what they
call 'the centre of the world'*. On this theory, the world stands
fast without any impacts from without, and top and bottom
cannot be parted in any direction, because everything has
been tending towards the centre – if you can believe that
anything rests upon itself. Whatever heavy bodies there
may be under the earth must then tend upwards and rest
against the surface upside down, like the images of things
which we now see reflected in water. In the same way they
would have it that animals walk about topsy-turvy and cannot fall off the earth into the nether quarters of the sky any
more than our bodies can soar up spontaneously into the
heavenly regions. When they are looking at the sun, we see
the stars of night; so they share the hours with us alternately
and experience nights corresponding to our days. But this is
an idle fancy of fools who have got hold of the wrong end
of the stick. There can be no centre in infinity. And, even if
there were, nothing could stand fast there rather than flee
from it. For all place or space, at the centre no less than
elsewhere, must give way to heavy bodies, no matter in
what direction they are moving. There is no place to which
bodies can come where they lose the property of weight and
stand still in the void. And vacuum cannot stand in the way
of anything so as not to allow it free passage, as its own
nature demands. Therefore things cannot be held in combination by this means through surrender to a craving for the
centre.

Besides, they do not claim that all bodies have this
tendency towards the centre, but only those of moisture

and earth – the waters of the deep and the floods that pour down from the hills and in general whatever is composed of a more or less earthy body. But according to their teaching the light breaths of air and hot fires are simultaneously wafted outwards away from the centre. The reason why the encircling ether twinkles with stars and the sun feeds its flames in the blue pastures of the sky is supposed to be that fire all congregates there in its flight from the centre. Similarly, the topmost branches of trees could not break into leaf unless their food had this same upward urge. But, if you allow matter to escape from the world in this way, you are leaving the ramparts of the world at liberty to crumble of a sudden and take flight with the speed of flame into the boundless void. The rest will follow. The thunder-breeding quarters of the sky will rush down from aloft. The ground will fall away from our feet, its particles dissolved amid the mingled wreckage of heaven and earth. The whole world will vanish into the abyss, and in the twinkling of an eye no remnant will be left but empty space and invisible atoms. At whatever point you first allow matter to fall short, this will be the gateway to perdition. Through this gate the whole concourse of matter will come streaming out.

If you take a little trouble, you will attain to a thorough understanding of these truths. For one thing will be illumined by another, and eyeless night will not rob you of your road till you have looked into the heart of nature's darkest mysteries. So surely will facts throw light upon facts.

Book II

MOVEMENTS AND SHAPES OF ATOMS

★

WHAT joy it is, when out at sea the stormwinds are lashing the waters, to gaze from the shore at the heavy stress some other man is enduring! Not that anyone's afflictions are in themselves a source of delight; but to realize from what troubles you yourself are free is joy indeed. What joy, again, to watch opposing hosts marshalled on the field of battle when you have yourself no part in their peril! But this is the greatest joy of all: to stand aloof in a quiet citadel, stoutly fortified by the teaching of the wise, and to gaze down from that elevation on others wandering aimlessly in a vain search for the way of life, pitting their wits one against another, disputing for precedence, struggling night and day with unstinted effort to scale the pinnacles of wealth and power. O joyless hearts of men! O minds without vision! How dark and dangerous the life in which this tiny span is lived away! Do you not see that nature is clamouring for two things only, a body free from pain, a mind released from worry and fear for the enjoyment of pleasurable sensations?

So we find that the requirements of our bodily nature are few indeed, no more than is necessary to banish pain. To heap pleasure upon pleasure may heighten men's enjoyment at times. But what matter if there are no golden images of youths about the house, holding flaming torches in their right hands to illumine banquets prolonged into the night?

What matter if the hall does not sparkle with silver and gleam with gold, and no carved and gilded rafters ring to the music of the lute? Nature does not miss these luxuries when men recline in company on the soft grass by a running stream under the branches of a tall tree and refresh their bodies pleasurably at small expense. Better still if the weather smiles upon them and the season of the year stipples the green herbage with flowers. Burning fevers flee no swifter from your body if you toss under figured counterpanes and coverlets of crimson than if you must lie in rude homespun.

If our bodies are not profited by treasures or titles or the majesty of kingship, we must go on to admit that neither are our minds. Or tell me, Memmius, when you see your legions thronging the Campus Martius in the ardour of mimic warfare, supported by ample auxiliaries, magnificently armed and fired by a common purpose, does that sight scare the terrors of superstition from your mind? Does the fear of death retire from your breast and leave it carefree at the moment when you sight your warships ranging far and wide? Or do we not find such resources absurdly ineffective? The fears and anxieties that dog the human breast do not shrink from the clash of arms or the fierce rain of missiles. They stalk unabashed among princes and potentates. They are not awe-struck by the gleam of gold or the bright sheen of purple robes.

Can you doubt then that this power rests with reason alone? All life is a struggle in the dark. As children in blank darkness tremble and start at everything, so we in broad daylight are oppressed at times by fears as baseless as those horrors which children imagine coming upon them in the dark. This dread and darkness of the mind cannot be dispelled by the sunbeams, the shining shafts of day, but only by an understanding of the outward form and inner workings of nature.

And now to business. I will explain *the motion by which the generative bodies of matter give birth to various things*, and, after they are born, dissolve them once more; the force that compels them to do this; and the power of movement through the boundless void with which they are endowed. It is for you to devote yourself attentively to my words.

Be sure that matter does not stick together in a solid mass. For we see that everything grows less and seems to melt away with the lapse of time and withdraw its old age from our eyes. And yet we see no diminution in the sum of things. This is because the bodies that are shed by one thing lessen it by their departure but enlarge another by their coming; here they bring decay, there full bloom, but they do not linger there. So the sum of things is perpetually renewed. Mortals live by mutual interchange. One race increases by another's decrease. The generations of living things pass in swift succession and like runners hand on the torch of life.

If you think that the atoms can stop and by their stopping generate new motions in things, you are wandering far from the path of truth. Since the atoms are moving freely through the void, they must all be kept in motion either by their own weight or on occasion by the impact of another atom. For it must often happen that two of them in their course knock together and immediately bounce apart in opposite directions, a natural consequence of their hardness and solidity and the absence of anything behind to stop them.

As a further indication that all particles of matter are on the move, remember that the universe is bottomless: there is no place where the atoms could come to rest. As I have already shown by various arguments and proved conclusively,

space is without end or limit and spreads out immeasurably
in all directions alike.

It clearly follows that no rest is given to the atoms in their
course through the depths of space. Driven along in an
incessant but variable movement, some of them bounce far
apart after a collision while others recoil only a short
distance from the impact. From those that do not recoil far,
being driven into a closer union and held there by the
entanglement of their own interlocking shapes, are composed firmly rooted rock, the stubborn strength of steel and
the like. Those others that move freely through larger tracts
of space, springing far apart and carried far by the rebound –
these provide for us thin air and blazing sunlight. Besides
these, there are many other atoms at large in empty space
which have been thrown out of compound bodies and have
nowhere even been granted admittance so as to bring their
motions into harmony.

This process, as I might point out, is illustrated by an
image of it that is continually taking place before our very
eyes. Observe what happens when sunbeams are admitted
into a building and shed light on its shadowy places. You
will see a multitude of tiny particles mingling in a multitude
of ways in the empty space within the light of the beam, as
though contending in everlasting conflict, rushing into battle
rank upon rank with never a moment's pause in a rapid
sequence of unions and disunions. From this you may picture
what it is for the atoms to be perpetually tossed about in the
illimitable void. To some extent a small thing may afford an
illustration and an imperfect image of great things. Besides,
there is a further reason why you should give your mind to
these particles that are seen dancing in a sunbeam: their
dancing is an actual indication of underlying movements of
matter that are hidden from our sight. There you will see

many particles under the impact of invisible blows changing their course and driven back upon their tracks, this way and that, in all directions. You must understand that they all derive this restlessness from the atoms. It originates with the atoms, which move of themselves. Then those small compound bodies that are least removed from the impetus of the atoms are set in motion by the impact of their invisible blows and in turn cannon against slightly larger bodies. So the movement mounts up from the atoms and gradually emerges to the level of our senses, so that those bodies are in motion that we see in sunbeams, moved by blows that remain invisible.

And now, Memmius, as to the rate at which the atoms move, you may gauge this readily from these few indications. First, when dawn sprays the earth with new-born light and the birds, flitting through pathless thickets, fill the neighbourhood according to their kind with liquid notes that glide through the thin air, it is plain and palpable for all to see how suddenly the sun at the moment of his rising drenches and clothes the world with his radiance. But the heat and the bright light which the sun emits do not travel through empty space. Therefore they are forced to move more slowly, cleaving their way as it were through waves of air. And the atoms that compose this radiance do not travel as isolated individuals but linked and massed together. Thus their pace is retarded by one dragging back another as well as by external obstacles. But, when separate atoms are travelling in solitary solidity through empty space, they encounter no obstruction from without and move as single units on the course on which they have embarked. Obviously therefore they must far outstrip the sunlight in speed of movement and traverse an extent of space many times as great in the time it takes for the sun's rays to flash across the sky. No wonder that men cannot follow the individual atoms, so as to discern the agency by which everything is brought about.

In the face of these truths, some people who know nothing of matter believe that nature without the guidance of the gods could not bring round the changing seasons in such perfect conformity to human needs, creating the crops and those other blessings that mortals are led to enjoy by the guide of life, divine pleasure, which coaxes them through the arts of Venus to reproduce their kind, lest the human race should perish. Obviously, in imagining that the gods established everything for the sake of men, they have stumbled in all respects far from the path of truth. Even if I knew nothing of the atoms, I would venture to assert on the evidence of the celestial phenomena themselves, supported by many other arguments, that the universe was certainly not created for us by divine power: it is so full of imperfections. All this, Memmius, I will elucidate for you at a later stage. Now let me complete my account of atomic movements.

Now, I should judge, is the place to insert a demonstration that *no material thing can be uplifted or travel upwards by its own power*. Do not be misled by the particles that compose flame. The fact that all weights taken by themselves tend downwards does not prevent lusty crops and trees from being born with an upward thrust and from growing and increasing upwards. Similarly, when fires leap up to the house-tops and devour beams and rafters with rapid flame, it must not be supposed that they do this of their own accord with no force to fling them up. Their behaviour is like that of blood released from our body when it spouts forth and springs aloft in a gory fountain. Observe also with what force beams and rafters are heaved up by water. The more we have shoved them down into the depths, many of us struggling strenuously together to push them under, the more eagerly the water spews and ejects them back again, so that more than half their bulk shoots up above the surface. And yet, I should judge, we have no doubt that all these, taken by themselves, would move downwards through empty space. It must be just the same with flames: under pressure they can shoot up through the gusty air, although their weight, taken by itself, strives to tug them down. Observe how the nocturnal torches of the sky in their lofty flight draw in their wake long trails of flame in whatever direction nature has set their course. See how stars and meteors fall upon the earth. The sun from the summit of the sky scatters heat in all directions and sows the fields with light. The sun's radiance therefore tends also towards the earth. Note again how the lightning flies through the rain-storms aslant. The fires that break out of the clouds rush together, now this way, now that; often enough the fiery force falls upon the earth.

In this connexion there is another fact that I want you to grasp. *When the atoms are travelling straight down through empty space by their own weight, at quite indeterminate times and places they swerve ever so little from their course,* just so much that you can call it a change of direction. If it were not for this swerve, everything would fall downwards like rain-drops through the abyss of space. No collision would take place and no impact of atom on atom would be created. Thus nature would never have created anything.

If anyone supposes that heavier atoms on a straight course through empty space could outstrip lighter ones and fall on them from above, thus causing impacts that might give rise

to generative motions, he is going far astray from the path
of truth. The reason why objects falling through water or
thin air vary in speed according to their weight is simply
that the matter composing water or air cannot obstruct all
objects equally, but is forced to give way more speedily to
heavier ones. But empty space can offer no resistance to any
object in any quarter at any time, so as not to yield free
passage as its own nature demands. Therefore, through
undisturbed vacuum all bodies must travel at equal speed
though impelled by unequal weights. The heavier will never
be able to fall on the lighter from above or generate of
themselves impacts leading to that variety of motions out of
which nature can produce things. We are thus forced back
to the conclusion that the atoms swerve a little – but only a
very little, or we shall be caught imagining slantwise movements, and the facts will prove us wrong. For we see plainly
and palpably that weights, when they come tumbling down,
have no power of their own to move aslant, so far as meets
the eye. But who can possibly perceive that they do not
diverge in the very least from a vertical course?

Again, if all movement is always interconnected, the new
arising from the old in a determinate order – if the atoms
never swerve so as to originate some new movement that
will snap the bonds of fate, the everlasting sequence of cause
and effect – what is the source of the free will possessed by
living things throughout the earth? What, I repeat, is the
source of that will-power snatched from the fates, whereby
we follow the path along which we are severally led by
pleasure, swerving from our course at no set time or place
but at the bidding of our own hearts? There is no doubt that
on these occasions the will of the individual originates the
movements that trickle through his limbs. Observe, when
the starting barriers are flung back, how the race-horses in

the eagerness of their strength cannot break away as suddenly as their hearts desire. For the whole supply of matter must first be mobilized throughout every member of the body: only then, when it is mustered in a continuous array, can it respond to the prompting of the heart. So you may see that the beginning of movement is generated by the heart; starting from the voluntary action of the mind, it is then transmitted throughout the body and the limbs. Quite different is our experience when we are shoved along by a blow inflicted with compulsive force by someone else. In that case it is obvious that all the matter of our body is set going and pushed along involuntarily, till a check is imposed through the limbs by the will. Do you see the difference? Although many men are driven by an external force and often constrained involuntarily to advance or to rush headlong, yet there is within the human breast something that can fight against this force and resist it. At its command the supply of matter is forced to take a new course through our limbs and joints or is checked in its course and brought once more to a halt. So also in the atoms you must recognize the same possibility: besides weight and impact there must be a third cause of movement, the source of this inborn power of ours, since we see that nothing can come out of nothing. For the weight of an atom prevents its movements from being completely determined by the impact of other atoms. But the fact that the mind itself has no internal necessity to determine its every act and compel it to suffer in helpless passivity – this is due to the slight swerve of the atoms at no determinate time or place.

The supply of matter in the universe was never more tightly packed than it is now, or more widely spaced out. For nothing is ever added to it or subtracted from it. It follows that the movement of atoms to-day is no different from what it was in bygone ages and always will be. So the things that have regularly come into being will continue to come into being in the same manner; they will be and grow and flourish so far as each is allowed by the laws of nature. The sum of things cannot be changed by any force. For there is no place into which any kind of matter might escape out of the universe or out of which some newly risen force could break into the universe and transform the whole nature of things and reverse their movements.

In this connexion there is one fact that need occasion no surprise. *Although all the atoms are in motion, their totality appears to stand totally motionless*, except for such movements as particular objects may make with their own bodies. This is because the atoms all lie far below the range of our senses. Since they are themselves invisible, their movements also must elude observation. Indeed, even visible objects, when set at a distance, often disguise their movements. Often on a hillside fleecy sheep, as they crop their lush pasture, creep slowly onward, lured this way or that by grass that sparkles with fresh dew, while the full-fed lambs gaily frisk and butt. And yet, when we gaze from a distance, we see only a blur – a white patch stationary on the green hillside. Take another example. Mighty legions, waging mimic war, are thronging the plain with their manoeuvres. The dazzling sheen flashes to the sky and all around the earth is ablaze with bronze. Down below there sounds the tramp of a myriad marching feet. A noise of shouting strikes upon the hills and reverberates to the celestial vault. Wheeling horsemen gallop hot-foot across the midst of the plain, till it quakes under the fury of their charge. And yet there is a vantage-ground

high among the hills from which all these appear immobile –
a blaze of light stationary upon the plain.

And now let us turn to a new theme – *the characteristics of the
atoms of all substances, the extent to which they differ in shape and
the rich multiplicity of their forms.* Not that there are not many
of the same shape, but they are by no means all identical
with one another. And no wonder. When the multitude of
them, as I have shown, is such that it is without limit or
count, it is not to be expected that they should all be
identical in build and configuration.

Consider the race of men, the scaly fish that swim in
silence, the lusty herds, the creatures of the wild and the
various feathered breeds, those that throng the vivifying
watery places, by river banks and springs and lakes, and
those that flock and flutter through pathless woodlands.
Take a representative of any of these diverse species and you
will still find that it differs in form from others of its kind.
Otherwise the young could not recognize their mother, nor
the mother her young. But we see that this can happen, and
that individuals of these species are mutually recognizable
no less than human beings.

Here is a familiar instance. Outside some stately fane of
the gods incense is smouldering on the altar. Beside it a
slaughtered calf falls to the ground. From its throat gushes a
hot stream of blood. But the bereaved dam, roaming through
green glades, scans the ground for the twin-pitted imprint
of familiar feet. Her eyes rove this way and that in search
of the missing young one. She pauses and fills the leafy
thickets with her plaints. Time and again she returns to the
byre, sore at heart with yearning for her calf. Succulent
osiers and herbage fresh with dew and her favourite streams
flowing level with their banks—all these are powerless to

console her and banish her new burden of distress. The sight
of other calves in the lush pastures is powerless to distract
her mind or relieve it of distress. So obvious is it that she
misses something distinctive and recognized.

In like manner, baby kids hail their own long-horned
dams with quavering voices. Frisky lambs pick out their own
mothers from the bleating flock. So at nature's bidding, each
runs to its own milk-swollen udder.

Among ears of corn, whatever the kind, you will not find
one just like another; but each will be marked by some
distinctive feature. The same holds good of the various
shells we see adorning the bosom of the land where the sea
with pliant ripples laps on the thirsty sands of its winding
shore. Here, then, is proof upon proof that in the stream of
atoms likewise, since they exist by nature and are not hand-
made to a fixed pattern, there are certain individual
differences of shape.

On this principle it is quite easy to explain why the fire
of lightning is far more penetrative than our fire which
springs from earthly torches. You can say that the heavenly
fire of the lightning is of finer texture, being composed of
smaller atoms, and can therefore pass through apertures
impervious to this fire of ours, which springs from wood
and is generated by a torch. Again, light passes through
horn, but rain is dashed back. Why, if not because the
particles of light are smaller than those that form the life-
giving drops of water? We see that wine flows through a
strainer as fast as it is poured in; but sluggish oil loiters.
This, no doubt, is either because oil consists of larger atoms,
or because these are more hooked and intertangled and,
therefore, cannot separate as rapidly, so as to trickle through
the holes one by one.

Here is a further example. Honey and milk, when they

are rolled in the mouth, cause an agreeable sensation to the tongue. But bitter wormwood and astringent centaury screw the mouth awry with their nauseating savour. You may readily infer that such substances as agreeably titillate the senses are composed of smooth round atoms. Those that seem bitter and harsh are more tightly compacted of hooked particles and accordingly tear their way into our senses and rend our bodies by their inroads.

The same conflict between two types of structure applies to everything that strikes the senses as good or bad. You cannot suppose that the rasping stridulation of a screeching saw is formed of elements as smooth as the notes a minstrel's nimble fingers wake from the lyre-strings and mould to melody. You cannot suppose that atoms of the same shape are entering our nostrils when stinking corpses are roasting as when the stage is freshly sprinkled with saffron of Cilicia and a near-by altar exhales the perfumes of the Orient. You cannot attribute the same composition to sights that feast the eye with colour and to those that make it smart and weep or that appear loathsome and repulsive through sheer ugliness. Nothing that gratifies the senses is ever without a certain smoothness of the constituent atoms. Whatever, on the other hand, is painful and harsh is characterized by a certain roughness of matter. Besides these there are some things that are not properly regarded as smooth but yet are not jagged with barbed spikes. These are characterized instead by slightly jutting ridges such as tickle the senses rather than hurt them. They include such things as wine-lees and piquant endive. Hot fire, again, and cold frost stab the senses of our body with teeth of a different pattern, as we learn from the different way they affect our sense of touch. For touch and nothing but touch (by all that men call holy!) is the essence of all our bodily sensations, whether we feel

something slipping in from outside or are hurt by something
born in the body or pleasantly excited by something going
out in the generative act of Venus. It is touch again that is
felt when the atoms are jarred by a knock so that they are
disordered and upset the senses : strike any part of your
own body with your hand, and you will experience this for
yourself. There must, therefore, be great differences in the
shapes of the atoms to provoke these different sensations.

Again, things that seem to us hard and stiff must be composed of deeply indented and hooked atoms and held firm
by their intertangling branches. In the front rank of this
class stand diamonds, with their steadfast indifference to
blows. Next come stout flints and stubborn steel and bronze
that stands firm with shrieking protest when the bolt is shot.
Liquids, on the other hand, must owe their fluid consistency
to component atoms that are smooth and round. For poppy-
seed can be poured as easily as if it were water; the globules
do not hold one another back, and when they are jolted they
tend to roll downhill as water does. A third class is constituted by things that you may see dissipated instantaneously,
such as smoke, clouds and flames. If their atoms are not all
smooth and round, yet they cannot be jagged and intertangled. They must be such as to prick the body and even to
penetrate rocks but not to stick together; so you can readily
grasp that substances hurtful to the senses but not solid are
sharp-pointed but without projections.

Do not be surprised to find that some things are both
bitter and fluid as, for instance, sea-water. This, being fluid,
consists of smooth round atoms. It causes pain because of
the admixture of many rough ones. There is no need for
these to be held together by hooks. Evidently they are
spherical as well as rough, so that they can roll round and
yet hurt the senses. It can be shown that Neptune's bitter

brine results from a mixture of rougher atoms with smooth.
There is a way of separating the two ingredients and viewing
them in isolation by filtering the sweet fluid through many
layers of earth so that it flows out into a pit and loses its
tang. It leaves behind the atoms of unpalatable brine because
owing to their roughness they are more apt to stick fast in
the earth.

To the foregoing demonstration I will link on another fact
which will gain credence from this context: *the number of
different forms of atoms is finite.* If it were not so, some of the
atoms would have to be of infinite magnitude. Within the
narrow limits of any single particle, there can be only a
limited range of forms. Suppose that atoms consist of three
minimum parts, or enlarge them by a few more. When by
fitting on parts at top or bottom and transposing left and
right you have exhausted every shape that can be given to
the whole body by all possible arrangements of the parts,
you are obviously left with no means of varying its form
further except by adding other parts. Thence it will follow,
if you wish to vary its form still further, that the arrangement will demand still other parts in exactly the same way.
Variation in shape goes with increase in size. You cannot
believe, therefore, that the atoms are distinguished by an
infinity of forms; or you will compel some of them to be of
enormous magnitude, which I have already proved to be
demonstrably impossible.

Were it not so, the richest robes of the Orient, resplendent with the Meliboean purple of Thessalian murex, or the
gilded breed of peacocks, gay with laughing lustre, would
pale before some new colour in things. The fragrance of
myrrh and the flavour of honey would fall into contempt.
The death-notes of the swan and the intricate melody of

Phoebus' lyre would be silenced in like manner. For whatever might be would always be surpassed by something more excellent. And, as all good things might yield to better, so might bad to worse. One thing would always be surpassed by another more offensive to nose or ear or eye or palate. Since this is not so, but things are bound by a set limit at either extreme, you must acknowledge a corresponding limit to the different forms of matter. Similarly there is a limited range, from fire to the icy frosts of winter and back again. There are extremes of heat and cold, and the intermediate temperatures complete the series. They have been created, therefore, a limited distance apart, since the extremes are marked at either end with two points, one made intolerable by flames, the other by congealing frosts.

To the foregoing demonstration I will link on another fact, which will gain credence from this context: *the number of atoms of any one form is infinite.* Since the varieties of form are limited, the number of uniform atoms must be unlimited. Otherwise the totality of matter would be finite, which I have proved in my verses is not so. I have shown that the universe is kept going by an infinite succession of atoms, so that the chain of impacts from all directions remains unbroken.

You may object that certain species of animals appear to be relatively rare, so that nature seems less well stocked with their seeds. But some other zone or environment in lands remote may abound in these, so as to make good the deficiency. As the outstanding instance among quadrupeds, we may note the snaky-handed elephants. Countless thousands of these must have gone to the making of that impenetrable ivory wall with which India is barricaded. Such is the abundance of these beasts, of which we see only very few samples.

Let us suppose for argument's sake that one unique object exists, with a body formed by birth – an object unlike anything else in the whole world. Unless there is an infinite supply of matter from which, once conceived, it can be brought to birth, it will have no chance even of being created, no prospect of further growth or replenishment. Let us further assume that a finite number of atoms generative of one particular thing are at large in the universe. What then will be the source or scene, the agency or mode, of their encounter in this multitudinous ocean of matter, this welter of foreign bodies? I see no possible means by which they could come together. Consider, when some great flotilla has been wrecked, how the mighty deep scatters floating wreckage – thwarts and ribs, yard-arms and prows, masts and sweeps; how stern-posts are seen adrift off the shores of every land – a warning to mortals to shun the stealth and violence and cunning of the treacherous sea and put no faith at any season in the false alluring laughter of that smooth still surface. Just so will your finite class of atoms, if once you posit such a thing, be scattered and tossed about through all eternity by conflicting tides of matter. They could never be swept together so as to enter into combination; nor could they remain combined or grow by increment. Yet experience plainly shows that both these things happen: objects can be born, and after birth they can grow. It is evident, therefore, that there are infinite atoms of every kind to keep up the supply of everything.

The destructive motions can never permanently get the upper hand and entomb vitality for evermore. Neither can

the generative and augmentative motions permanently safeguard what they have created. So the war of the elements
that has raged throughout eternity continues on equal
terms. Now here, now there, the forces of life are victorious
and in turn vanquished. With the voice of mourning
mingles the cry that infants raise when their eyes open on
the sunlit world. Never has day given place to night or
night to dawn that has not heard, blent with these infant
wailings, the lamentation that attends on death and sombre
obsequies.

In this connexion there is one fact that you should keep
signed and sealed and recorded in the archives of memory:
there is no visible object that consists of atoms of one kind only.
Everything is composed of a mixture of elements. The
more qualities and powers a thing possesses, the greater
variety it attests in the forms of its component atoms.

In the first place the earth contains in itself the atoms
with which the measureless ocean is perpetually renewed
by streams that roll down coolness. It also contains matter
from which fires can arise: in many places the soil is set
alight and burns, and subterranean fires sustain the furious
outrush of Etna. It contains in addition the stores out of
which it can thrust up thriving crops and lusty orchard
trees for the races of men and provide rivers and foliage and
lush pasture for the wild beasts of the mountain. That is
why this one being has earned such titles as Great Mother
of the Gods, Mother of Beasts and progenitress of the
human frame.

This is she who was hymned by Grecian poets adept in
ancient lore. They pictured her a goddess, driving a chariot
drawn by a yoke of lions. By this they signified that the
whole mighty mass hangs in airy space: for earth cannot

rest on earth. They harnessed wild beasts, because the
fiercest of children cannot but be softened and subdued by
the duty owed to parents. Upon her head they set a battle-
mented crown, because earth in select spots is fortified and
bears the weight of cities. Decked with this emblem even
now the image of the Holy Mother is borne about the world
in solemn state. Various nations hail her with time-
honoured ceremony as our Lady of Ida. To bear her company they appoint a Phrygian retinue, because they claim
that crops were first created within the bounds of Phrygia
and spread thence throughout the earth. They give her
eunuchs as attendant priests, to signify that those who have
defied their mother's will and shown ingratitude to their
father must be counted unworthy to bring forth living
children into the sunlit world. A thunder of drums attends
her, tight-stretched and pounded by palms, and a clash of
hollow cymbals; hoarse-throated horns bray their deep
warning, and the pierced flute thrills every heart with
Phrygian strains. Weapons are carried before her, symbolic
of rabid frenzy, to chasten the thankless and profane hearts
of the rabble with dread of her divinity. So, when first she
is escorted into some great city and mutely enriches
mortals with wordless benediction, they strew her path all
along the route with a lavish largesse of copper and silver
and shadow the Mother and her retinue with a snow of
roses. Next an armed band, whom the Greeks call Phrygian
Curetes, joust together and join in rhythmic dances, merry
with blood and nodding their heads to set their terrifying
crests aflutter. They call to mind those Curetes of Dicté,
who once on a time in Crete, as the story goes, drowned the
wailing of the infant Jove by dancing with swift feet, an
armed band of boys around a boy, and rhythmically clashing
bronze on bronze, lest Saturn should seize and crush him in

his jaws and deal his mother's heart a wound that would not heal. That perhaps is why they attend in arms upon the Great Mother. Or else they signify that the goddess bids men be ready to defend their native earth staunchly by force of arms and resolve to shield their parents and do them credit. It may be claimed that all this is aptly and admirably devised. It is nevertheless far removed from the truth. For it is essential to the very nature of deity that it should enjoy immortal existence in utter tranquillity, aloof and detached from our affairs. It is free from all pain and peril, strong in its own resources, exempt from any need of us, indifferent to our merits and immune from anger.

If anyone elects to call the sea Neptune and the crops Ceres and would rather take Bacchus' name in vain than denote grape juice by its proper title, we may allow him to refer to the earth as the Mother of the Gods, provided that he genuinely refrains from polluting his mind with the foul taint of superstition. In fact, the earth is and always has been an insentient being. The reason why it sends up countless products in countless ways into the sunlight is simply that it contains atoms of countless substances.

It often happens that fleecy flocks and martial steeds and horned cattle crop the herbage of a single field under the same canopy of sky and quench their thirst with the water of a single stream; yet they live according to their own kind and severally keep the nature of their parents and copy their behaviour. So varied is the store of matter in every sort of herb and in every stream.

Furthermore every individual animal of any species is a whole composed of various parts – bones, blood, veins, heat, moisture, flesh, sinews; and these are all widely different, being formed of differently shaped atoms. Again, whatever can be set on fire and burnt must conceal in its body, if nothing else, at least the matter needed for emitting fire and radiating light, for shooting out sparks and scattering abroad ashes. If you mentally examine anything else by a similar procedure, you will find that it hides in its body the seeds of many substances and combines atoms of various forms.

You see that many objects are possessed of colour and taste together with smell. Their component matter must therefore be multiform. For scent penetrates the human frame where tint does not go; tint creeps into the senses by a different route from taste. So you may infer that they differ in their atomic forms. Different shapes therefore combine in a single mass, and objects are composed of a mixture of seeds. Consider how in my verses, for instance, you see many letters common to many words; yet you must admit that different verses and words are composed of different letters. Not that there is any lack of letters common to several words, or that there are no two words composed of precisely the same letters; but they do not all alike consist of exactly the same components. So in other things, although many atoms are common to many substances, yet these substances may still differ in their composition. So it can rightly be said that the human race differs in its composition from crops or orchard trees.

It must not be supposed that atoms of every sort can be linked in every variety of combination. If that were so, you would see monsters coming into being everywhere. Hybrid growths of man and beast would arise. Lofty branches would sprout here and there from a living body. Limbs of land-beast and sea-beast would often be conjoined. Chimaeras breathing flame from hideous jaws would be reared by nature throughout the all-generating earth. But it is evident that nothing of this sort happens. We see that everything is created from specific seeds and born of a specific mother and grows up true to type. We may infer that this is determined by some specific necessity. In every individual the atoms of its own kind, derived from all its food, disperse through its limbs and link together so as to set going the appropriate motions. But we see extraneous matter cast back by nature into the earth; and much is expelled from the body, under the impact of blows, in the form of invisible particles which could not link on anywhere or harmonize with the vital motions within so as to copy them.

Do not imagine that these laws are binding on animals alone. The same principle determines everything. As all created things differ from one another by their entire natures, so each one must necessarily consist of distinctive forms of atoms. Not that there is any lack of atoms of the same forms; but objects do not all alike consist of exactly the same components. Since the seeds are not identical, they must differ in their intervals, paths, attachments, weights, impacts, clashes and motions. These do not merely distinguish one animal body from another but separate land from sea and hold the whole sky apart from the earth.

Give ear now to arguments that I have searched out with an effort that was also a delight. Do not imagine that white objects derive the snowy aspect they present to your eyes from white atoms, or that black objects are composed of a black element. And in general do not believe that anything owes the colour it displays to the fact that its atoms are tinted correspondingly. *The primary particles of matter have no colour whatsoever*, neither the same colour as the objects they compose nor a different one. If you think the mind cannot lay hold of such bodies, you are quite wrong. Men who are blind from birth and have never looked on the sunlight have knowledge by touch of bodies that have never from the beginning been associated with any colour. It follows that on our minds also an image can impinge of bodies not marked by any tint. Indeed the things that we ourselves touch in pitch darkness are not felt by us as possessing any colour.

Having proved that colourless bodies are not unthinkable, I will proceed to demonstrate that the atoms must be such bodies.

First, then, any colour may change completely to any other. But the atoms cannot possibly change colour. For something must remain changeless, or everything would be absolutely annihilated. For, if ever anything is so transformed as to overstep its own limits, this means the immediate death of what was before. So do not stain the atoms with colour, or you will find everything slipping back into nothing.

Let us suppose, then, that the atoms are naturally colourless and that it is through the variety of their shapes that they produce the whole range of colours, a great deal depending on their combinations and positions and their reciprocal motions. You will now find it easy to explain without more ado why things that were dark-coloured a moment since can suddenly become as white as marble – as the sea, for instance, when its surface is ruffled by a fresh breeze, is turned into white wave-crests of marble lustre. You could say that something we often see as dark is promptly transformed through the churning up of its matter and a reshuffling of atoms, with some additions and subtractions, so that it is seen as bleached and white. If, on the other hand, the waters of the sea were composed of blue atoms, they could not possibly be whitened; for, however

you may stir up blue matter, it can never change its colour
to the pallor of marble.

It might be supposed that the uniform lustre of the sea is
made up of particles of different colours, as for instance a
single object of a square shape is often made up of other
objects of various shapes. But in the square we discern the
different shapes. So in the surface of the sea or in any other
uniform lustre we ought, on this hypothesis, to discern a
variety of widely different colours. Besides, differences in
the shapes of the parts are no hindrance to the whole being
square in outline. But differences in colour completely
prevent it from displaying an unvariegated lustre.

The seductive argument that sometimes tempts us to
attribute colours to the atoms is demolished by the fact that
white objects are not created from white material nor black
from black, but both from various colours. Obviously,
white could much more readily spring from no colour at
all than from black, or from any other colour that interferes
and conflicts with it.

Again, since there can be no colours without light and
the atoms do not emerge into the light, it can be inferred
that they are not clothed in any colour. For what colour can
there be in blank darkness? Indeed, colour is itself changed
by a change of light, according as the beams strike it
vertically or aslant. Observe the appearance in sunlight of
the plumage that rings the neck of a dove and crowns its
nape: sometimes it is tinted with the brilliant red of a ruby;
at others it is seen from a certain point of view to mingle
emerald greens with the blue of the sky. In the same way a
peacock's tail, profusely illumined, changes colour as it is
turned this way or that. These colours, then, are created by
a particular incidence of light. Hence, no light, no colour.

When the pupil of the eye is said to perceive the colour

white, it experiences in fact a particular kind of impact. When it perceives black, or some other colour, the impact is different. But, when you touch things, it makes no odds what colour they may be, but only what is their shape. The inference is that the atoms have no need of colour, but cause various sensations of touch according to their various shapes.

Since there is no natural connexion between particular colours and particular shapes, atoms (if they were not colourless) might equally well be of any colour irrespective of their form. Why then are not their compounds tinted with every shade of colour irrespective of their kind? We should expect on this hypothesis that ravens in flight would often emit a snowy sheen from snowy wings; and that some swans would be black, being composed of black atoms, or would display some other uniform or variegated colour.

Again, the more anything is divided into tiny parts, the more you can see its colour gradually dimming and fading out. When red cloth, for instance, is pulled to pieces thread by thread, its crimson or scarlet colour, than which there is none brighter, is all dissipated. From this you may gather that, before its particles are reduced right down to atoms, they would shed all their colour.

Finally, since you acknowledge that not all objects emit noise or smell, you accept that as a reason for not attributing sounds and scents to everything. On the same principle, since we cannot perceive everything by eye, we may infer that some things are colourless, just as some things are scentless and soundless, and that these can be apprehended by the percipient mind as readily as things that are lacking in some other quality.

Do not imagine that colour is the only quality that is denied to the atoms. *They are also wholly devoid of warmth and cold and*

*scorching heat; they are barren of sound and starved of savour, and
emit no inherent odour from their bodies.* When you are setting
out to prepare a pleasant perfume of marjoram or myrrh or
flower of spikenard, breathing nectar into our nostrils, your
first task is to select so far as possible an oil that is naturally
odourless and sends out no exhalation to our nostrils. This
will be least liable to corrupt the scents blended and con-
cocted with its substance by contamination with its own
taint. For the same reason the atoms must not impart to
things at their birth a scent or sound that is their own
property, since they can send nothing out of themselves;
nor must they contribute any flavour or cold or heat,
whether scorching or mild, or anything else of the kind.

These qualities, again, are perishable things, made pliable
by the softness of their substance, breakable by its crumbli-
ness and penetrable by its looseness of texture. They must
be kept far apart from the atoms, if we wish to provide the
universe with imperishable foundations on which it may
rest secure; or else you will find everything slipping back
into nothing.

At this stage you must admit that *whatever is seen to be sentient
is nevertheless composed of atoms that are insentient.* The phenomena open to our observation do not contradict this conclusion or conflict with it. Rather, they lead us by the hand
and compel us to believe that the animate is born, as I
maintain, of the insentient.

As a particular instance, we can point to living worms,
emerging from foul dung when the earth is soaked and
rotted by intemperate showers. Besides, we see every sort
of substance transformed in the same way. Rivers, foliage
and lush pastures are transformed into cattle; the substance
of cattle is transformed into our bodies; and often enough

our bodies go to build up the strength of predatory beasts or the bodies of the lords of the air. So nature transforms all foods into living bodies and generates from them all the senses of animate creatures, just as it makes dry wood blossom out in flame and transfigures it wholly into fire. So now do you see that it makes a great difference in what order the various atoms are arranged and with what others they are combined so as to impart and take over motions?

What is it, then, that jogs the mind itself and moves and compels it to express certain sentiments, so that you do not believe that the sentient is generated by the insentient? Obviously it is the fact that a mixture of water and wood and earth cannot of itself bring about vital sensibility. There is one relevant point you should bear in mind: I am not maintaining that sensations are generated automatically from all the elements out of which sentient things are created. Everything depends on the size and shape of the sense-producing atoms and on their appropriate motions, arrangements and positions. None of these is found in wood or clods. And yet these substances, when they are fairly well rotted by showers, give birth to little worms, because the particles of matter are jolted out of their old arrangements by a new factor and combined in such a way that animate objects must result.

Again, those who would have it that sensation can be produced only by sensitive bodies, which originate in their turn from others similarly sentient – these theorists are making the foundations of our senses perishable, because they are making them soft. For sensitivity is always associated with flesh, sinews, veins – all things that we see to be soft and composed of perishable stuff.

Let us suppose, for argument's sake, that particles of these substances could endure everlastingly. The sensation with

which they are credited must be either that of a part or else
similar to that of an animate being as a whole. But it is
impossible for parts by themselves to experience sensation:
all the sensations felt in our limbs are felt by us as a whole;
a hand or any other member severed from the whole body
is quite powerless to retain sensation on its own. There
remains the alternative that such particles have senses like
those of an animate being as a whole. They must then feel
precisely what we feel, so as to share in all our vital sensations. How then can they pass for elements and escape the
path of death, since they are animate beings, and animate
and mortal are one and the same thing? Even supposing they
could escape death, yet they will make nothing by their
combination and conjunction but a mob or horde of living
things, just as men and cattle and wild beasts obviously
could not combine so as to give birth to a single thing. If
we suppose that they shed their own sentience from their
bodies and acquire another one, what is the point of giving
them the one that is taken away? Besides, as we saw before,
from the fact that we perceive eggs turning into live
fledgelings and worms swarming out when the earth has
been rotted by intemperate showers, we may infer that
sense can be generated from the insentient.

Suppose someone asserts that sense can indeed emerge
from the insentient, but only by some transformation or
some creative process comparable to birth. He will be
adequately answered by a clear demonstration that birth
and transformation occur only as the result of union or
combination. Admittedly sensation cannot arise in any body
until an animate creature has been born. This of course is
because the requisite matter is dispersed through air and
streams and earth and the products of earth: it has not come
together in the appropriate manner, so as to set in mutual

operation those vitalizing motions that kindle the all-watchful senses which keep watch over every animate creature.

When any animate creature is suddenly assailed by a more powerful blow than its nature can withstand, all the senses of body and mind are promptly thrown into confusion. For the juxtapositions of the atoms are unknit, and the vitalizing motions are inwardly obstructed, until the matter, jarred and jolted throughout every limb, loosens the vital knots of the spirit from the body and expels the spirit in scattered particles through every pore. What other effect can we attribute to the infliction of a blow than this of shaking and shattering everything to bits? Besides, it often happens, when the blow is less violently inflicted, that such vitalizing motions as survive emerge victorious; they assuage the immense upheavals resulting from the shock, recall every particle to its own proper courses, break up the lethal motion when it is all but master of the body and rekindle the well-nigh extinguished senses. How else could living creatures on the very threshold of death rally their consciousness and return to life rather than make good their departure by a route on which they have already travelled most of the way?

Again, pain occurs when particles of matter have been unsettled by some force within the living flesh of the limbs and stagger in their inmost stations. When they slip back into place, that is blissful pleasure. It follows that the atoms cannot be afflicted by any pain or experience any pleasure in themselves, since they are not composed of any primal particles, by some reversal of whose movements they might suffer anguish or reap some fruition of vitalizing bliss. They cannot therefore be endowed with any power of sensation.

Again, if we are to account for the power of sensation possessed by animate creatures in general by attributing sentience to their atoms, what of those atoms that specifically compose the human race? Presumably they are not merely sentient, but also shake their sides with uproarious guffaws and besprinkle their cheeks with dewy teardrops and even discourse profoundly and at length about the composition of the universe and proceed to ask of what elements they are themselves composed. If they are to be likened to entire mortals, they must certainly consist of other elemental particles, and these again of others. There is no point at which you may call a halt, but I will follow you there with your argument that whatever speaks or laughs or thinks is composed of particles that do the same. Let us acknowledge that this is stark madness and lunacy: one can laugh without being composed of laughing particles, can think and proffer learned arguments though sprung from seeds neither thoughtful nor eloquent. Why then cannot the things that we see gifted with sensation be compounded of seeds that are wholly senseless?

Lastly, we are all sprung from heavenly seed. All alike have the same father, from whom all-nourishing mother earth receives the showering drops of moisture. Thus fertilized, she gives birth to smiling crops and lusty trees, to mankind and all the breeds of beasts. She it is that yields the food on which they all feed their bodies, lead their joyous lives and renew their race. So she has well earned the name of mother. In like manner this matter returns: what came from earth goes back into the earth; what was sent down from the ethereal vault is readmitted to the precincts of heaven. Death does not put an end to things by annihilating the component particles but by breaking up their conjunction. Then it links them in new combinations,

making everything change in shape and colour and give up
in an instant its acquired gift of sensation. So you may
realize what a difference it makes in what combinations and
positions the same elements occur, and what motions they
mutually pass on and take over. You will thus avoid the
mistake of conceiving as permanent properties of the atoms
the qualities that are seen floating on the surface of things,
coming into being from time to time and as suddenly
perishing. Obviously it makes a great difference in these
verses of mine in what context and order the letters are
arranged. If not all, at least the greater part is alike. But
differences in their position distinguish word from word.
Just so with actual objects: when there is a change in the
combination, motion, order, position or shapes of the
component matter, there must be a corresponding change
in the object composed.

Give your mind now to the true reasoning I have to unfold.
A new fact is battling strenuously for access to your ears.
A new aspect of the universe is striving to reveal itself.
But no fact is so simple that it is not harder to believe than
to doubt at the first presentation. Equally, there is nothing
so mighty or so marvellous that the wonder it evokes does
not tend to diminish in time. Take first the pure and
undimmed lustre of the sky and all that it enshrines: the
stars that roam across its surface, the moon and the
surpassing splendour of the sunlight. If all these sights were
now displayed to mortal view for the first time by a swift
unforeseen revelation, what miracle could be recounted
greater than this? What would men before the revelation
have been less prone to conceive as possible? Nothing,
surely. So marvellous would have been that sight – a sight
which no one now, you will admit, thinks worthy of an

upward glance into the luminous regions of the sky. So
has satiety blunted the appetite of our eyes. Desist, therefore, from thrusting out reasoning from your mind because
of its disconcerting novelty. Weigh it, rather, with dis-
cerning judgment. Then, if it seems to you true, give in.
If it is false, gird yourself to oppose it. For the mind wants
to discover by reasoning what exists in the infinity of space
that lies out there, beyond the ramparts of this world – that
region into which the intellect longs to peer and into which
the free projection of the mind does actually extend its
flight.

Here, then, is my first point. In all dimensions alike, on
this side or that, upward or downward through the
universe, there is no end. This I have shown, and indeed the
fact proclaims itself aloud and the nature of space makes it
crystal clear. Granted, then, that empty space extends without limit in every direction and that seeds innumerable in
number are rushing on countless courses through an
unfathomable universe under the impulse of perpetual
motion, *it is in the highest degree unlikely that this earth and sky
is the only one to have been created* and that all those particles
of matter outside are accomplishing nothing. This follows
from the fact that our world has been made by nature
through the spontaneous and casual collision and the multifarious, accidental, random and purposeless congregation
and coalescence of atoms whose suddenly formed combinations could serve on each occasion as the starting-point of
substantial fabrics – earth and sea and sky and the races of
living creatures. On every ground, therefore, you must
admit that there exist elsewhere other congeries of matter
similar to this one which the ether clasps in ardent embrace.

When there is plenty of matter in readiness, when space
is available and no cause or circumstance impedes, then

surely things must be wrought and effected. You have a
store of atoms that could not be reckoned in full by the
whole succession of living creatures. You have the same
natural force to congregate them in any place precisely
as they have been congregated here. You are bound therefore to acknowledge that in other regions there are
other earths and various tribes of men and breeds of
beasts.

Add to this the fact that nothing in the universe is the
only one of its kind, unique and solitary in its birth and
growth; everything is a member of a species comprising
many individuals. Turn your mind first to the animals. You
will find the rule apply to the brutes that prowl the mountains, to the children of men, the voiceless scaly fish and all
the forms of flying things. So you must admit that sky, earth,
sun, moon, sea and the rest are not solitary, but rather
numberless. For a firmly established limit is set to their
lives also and their bodies also are a product of birth, no less
than that of any creature that flourishes here according
to its kind.

Bear this well in mind, and you will immediately perceive
that *nature is free and uncontrolled by proud masters* and runs
the universe by herself without the aid of gods. For who –
by the sacred hearts of the gods who pass their unruffled
lives, their placid aeon, in calm and peace! – who can rule
the sum total of the measureless? Who can hold in coercive
hand the strong reins of the unfathomable? Who can spin
all the firmaments alike and foment with the fires of ether
all the fruitful earths? Who can be in all places at all times,
ready to darken the clear sky with clouds and rock it with a
thunderclap – to launch bolts that may often wreck his own
temples, or retire and spend his fury letting fly at deserts

with that missile which often passes by the guilty and slays
the innocent and blameless?

After the natal season of the world, the birthday of sea and
lands and the uprising of the sun, many atoms have been
added from without, many seeds contributed on every side
by bombardment from the universe at large. From these the
sea and land could gather increase; the dome of heaven
could gain more room and lift its rafters high above the
earth, and the air could climb upwards. For to each are
allotted its own atoms from every quarter under the impact
of blows. They all rejoin their own kind: water goes to
water, earth swells with earthy matter; fire is forged by
fires, ether by ether. At length everything is brought to its
utmost limit of growth by nature, the creatress and per-
fectress. This is reached when what is poured into its vital
veins is no more than what flows and drains away. Here the
growing-time of everything must halt. Here nature checks
the increase of her own strength. The things you see growing merrily in stature and climbing step by step the stairs
of maturity – these are gaining more atoms than they lose.
The food is easily introduced into all their veins; and they
themselves are not so widely expanded as to shed much
matter and squander more than their age absorbs as
nourishment. It must, of course, be conceded that many
particles ebb and drain away from things. But more
particles must accrue, until they have touched the topmost
peak of growth. Thereafter the strength and vigour of
maturity is gradually broken, and age slides down the path
of decay. Obviously the bulkier anything is and the more
expanded when it begins to wane, the more particles it
sheds and gives off from every surface. The food is not easily
distributed through all its veins, or supplied in sufficient

quantities to make good the copious effluences it exudes.
For everything must be restored and renewed by food, and
by food buttressed and sustained. And the process is doomed
to failure, because the veins do not admit enough and nature
does not supply all that is needed. It is natural, therefore, that everything should perish when it is thinned out
by the ebbing of matter and succumbs to blows from
without. The food supply is no longer adequate for its
aged frame, and the deadly bombardment of particles
from without never pauses in the work of dissolution and
subdual.

In this way the ramparts of the great world also will be
breached and collapse in crumbling ruin about us. Already
it is far past its prime. The earth, which generated every
living species and once brought forth from its womb the
bodies of huge beasts, has now scarcely strength to generate
animalcules. For I assume that the races of mortal creatures
were not let down into the fields from heaven by a golden
cord, nor generated from the sea or the rock-beating surf,
but born of the same earth that now provides their nurture.
The same earth in her prime spontaneously generated for
mortals smiling crops and lusty vines, sweet fruits and
gladsome pastures, which now scarcely be made to grow
by our toil. We wear down the oxen and wear out the
strength of husbandmen, and the ploughshare is scarcely a
match for fields that grudge their fruits and multiply our
toil. Already the ploughman of ripe years shakes his head
with many a sigh that his heavy labours have gone for
nothing; and, when he compares the present with the past,
he often cries up his father's luck and grumbles that past
generations, when men were old-fashioned and god-fearing,
supported life easily enough on their small farms, though
one man's holding was then far less than now. In the same

despondent vein, the cultivator of old and wilted vines decries the trend of the times and rails at heaven. He does not realize that everything is gradually decaying and nearing its end, worn out by old age.

Book III

LIFE AND MIND

*

Y o u , who out of black darkness were first to lift up a shining light, revealing the hidden blessings of life – you are my
guide, O glory of the Grecian race. In your well-marked
footprints now I plant my resolute steps. It is from love
alone that I long to imitate you, not from emulous ambition.
Shall the swallow contend in song with the swan, or the kid
match its rickety legs in a race with the strong-limbed
steed? You are my father, illustrious discoverer of truth,
and give me a father's guidance. From your pages, as bees
in flowery glades sip every blossom, so do I crop all your
Golden Sayings – golden indeed, and for ever worthy of
everlasting life.

As soon as your reasoning, sprung from that god-like
mind, lifts up its voice to proclaim the nature of the universe, then the terrors of the mind take flight, the ramparts
of the world roll apart, and I see the march of events
throughout the whole of space. The majesty of the gods is
revealed and those quiet habitations, never shaken by storms
nor drenched by rain-clouds nor defaced by white drifts of
snow which a harsh frost congeals. A cloudless ether roofs
them, and laughs with radiance lavishly diffused. All their
wants are supplied by nature, and nothing at any time
cankers their peace of mind. But nowhere do I see the halls
of Hell, though the earth is no barrier to my beholding all
that passes underfoot in the space beneath. At this I am

seized with a divine delight, and a shuddering awe, that by your power nature stands thus unveiled and made manifest in every part.

I have already shown what the component bodies of everything are like; how they vary in shape; how they fly spontaneously through space, impelled by a perpetual motion; and how from these all objects can be created. The next step now is evidently to elucidate in my verses the nature of mind and of life. In so doing I shall drive out neck and crop that fear of Hell which blasts the life of man from its very foundations, sullying everything with the blackness of death and leaving no pleasure pure and unalloyed. I know that men often speak of sickness or of shameful life as more to be dreaded than the terrors of Hell; they profess to know that the mind consists of blood, or maybe wind, if that is how the whim takes them, and to stand in no need whatever of our reasoning. But all this talk is based more on a desire to show off than on actual proof, as you may infer from their conduct. These same men, though they may be exiled from home, banished far from the sight of their fellows, soiled with some filthy crime, a prey to every torment, still cling to life. Wherever they come in their tribulation, they make propitiatory sacrifices, slaughter black cattle and despatch offerings to the Departed Spirits. The heavier their afflictions, the more devoutly they turn their minds to superstition. Look at a man in the midst of doubt and danger, and you will learn in his hour of adversity what he really is. It is then that true utterances are wrung from the recesses of his breast. The mask is torn off; the reality remains.

Consider too the greed and blind lust of power that drive unhappy men to overstep the bounds of right and may even

turn them into accomplices or instruments of crime, struggling night and day with unstinted effort to scale the
pinnacles of wealth. These running sores of life are fed in no
small measure by the fear of death. For abject ignominy and
irksome poverty seem far indeed from the joy and assurance
of life, and in effect loitering already at the gateway of death.
From such a fate men revolt in groundless terror and long to
escape far, far away. So in their greed of gain they amass a
fortune out of civil bloodshed: piling wealth on wealth,
they heap carnage on carnage. With heartless glee they
welcome a brother's tragic death. They hate and fear the
hospitable board of their own kin. Often, in the same spirit
and influenced by the same fear, they are consumed with
envy at the sight of another's success: he walks in a blaze of
glory, looked up to by all, while they curse the dingy
squalor in which their own lives are bogged. Some sacrifice
life itself for the sake of statues and a title. Often from fear
of death mortals are gripped by such a hate of living and
looking on the light that with anguished hearts they do
themselves to death. They forget that this very fear is the
fountainhead of their troubles; this it is that harasses conscience, snaps the bonds of friendship and hurls down virtue
from the heights. Many a time before now men have
betrayed their country and their beloved parents in an effort
to escape the halls of Hell.

As children in blank darkness tremble and start at everything, so we in broad daylight are oppressed at times by
fears as baseless as those horrors which children imagine
coming upon them in the dark. This dread and darkness of
the mind cannot be dispelled by the sunbeams, the shining
shafts of day, but only by an understanding of the outward
form and inner workings of nature.

First, I maintain that *the mind*, which we often call the intellect, the seat of the guidance and control of life, *is part of a man*, no less than hand or foot or eyes are parts of a whole living creature. There are some who argue that the sentience of the mind is not lodged in any particular part, but is a vital condition of the body, what the Greeks call a *harmony*, which makes us live as sentient beings without having any locally determined mind. Just as good health may be said to belong to the healthy body without being any specific part of it, so they do not station the sentience of the mind in any specific part. In this they seem to me very wide of the mark. Often enough the visible body is obviously ill, while in some other unseen part we are enjoying ourselves. No less often the reverse happens: one who is sick at heart enjoys bodily well-being. This is no different from the experience of an invalid whose foot is hurting while his head is in no pain.

Or consider what happens when we have surrendered our limbs to soothing slumber and our body, replete and relaxed, lies insensible. At that very time there is something else in us that is awake to all sorts of stimuli – something that gives free admittance to all the motions of joy and to heart-burnings void of substance.

Next, you must understand that *there is also a vital spirit in our limbs* and the body does not derive its sentience from harmony. In the first place, life often lingers in our limbs after a large part of the body has been cut off. On the other hand, when a few particles of heat have dispersed and some air has been let out through the mouth, life forsakes the veins forthwith and abandons the bones. Hence you may infer that all the elements do not hold equal portions of vitality or sustain it equally, but it is chiefly thanks to the atoms of wind and heat that life lingers in the limbs. There is therefore in the body itself a vital breath and heat which forsakes our limbs at death.

Now that we have discovered the nature of the mind and of the vital spirit as a part of the man, drop this name harmony which was passed down to the musicians from the heights of Helicon – or else perhaps they fetched it themselves from some other source and applied it to the matter of their art, which had then no name of its own. Whatever it be, let them keep it. And give your attention now to the rest of my discourse.

Next, I maintain that *mind and spirit are interconnected* and compose between them a single substance. But what I may call the head and the dominant force in the whole body is that guiding principle which we term mind or intellect. This is firmly lodged in the mid-region of the breast. Here is the place where fear and alarm pulsate. Here is felt the caressing touch of joy. Here, then, is the seat of intellect and mind. The rest of the vital spirit, diffused throughout the body, obeys the mind and moves under its direction and impulse. The mind by itself experiences thought and joy of its own at a time when nothing moves either the body or the spirit.

When our head or eye suffers from an attack of pain, our whole body does not share in its aching. Just so the mind sometimes suffers by itself or jumps for joy when the rest of the spirit, diffused through every limb and member, is not stirred by any new impulse. But, when the mind is upset by some more overwhelming fear, we see all the spirit in every limb upset in sympathy. Sweat and pallor break out all over the body. Speech grows inarticulate; the voice fails; the eyes swim; the ears buzz; the limbs totter.

Often we see men actually drop down because of the terror that has gripped their minds. Hence you may readily infer a connexion between the mind and the spirit which, when shaken by the impact of the mind, immediately jostles and propels the body.

The same reasoning proves that *mind and spirit are both composed of matter*. We see them propelling the limbs, rousing the body from sleep, changing the expression of the face and guiding and steering the whole man – activities that all clearly involve touch, as touch in turn involves matter. How then can we deny their material nature? You see the mind sharing in the body's experiences and sympathizing with it. When the nerve-racking impact of a spear gashes bones and sinews, even if it does not penetrate to the seat of life, there ensues faintness and a tempting inclination earthwards and on the ground a turmoil in the mind and an intermittent faltering impulse to stand up again. The substance of the mind must therefore be material, since it is affected by the impact of material weapons.

My next task will be to demonstrate to you what sort of matter it is of which this mind is composed and how it was formed. First, I affirm that *it is of very fine texture and composed of exceptionally minute particles*. If you will mark my words, you will be able to infer this from the following facts. It is evident that nothing happens as quickly as the mind represents and sketches the happening to itself. Therefore the mind sets itself in motion more swiftly than any of those things whose substance is visible to our eyes. But what is so mobile must consist of exceptionally minute and spherical atoms, so that it can be set going by a slight push. The reason why water is set going and flowing by such

a slight push is of course the smallness of its atoms and their
readiness to roll. The stickier consistency of honey – its
relatively sluggish flow and dilatory progress – is due to the
closer coherence of the component matter, consisting, as it
obviously does, of particles not so smooth or so fine or so
round. A high pile of poppy seed can be disturbed by a light
puff of breeze, so that it trickles down from the top,
whereas a heap of stones or corn ears remains immovable.
In proportion as objects are smaller and smoother, so much
the more do they enjoy mobility; the greater their weight
and roughness, the more firmly are they anchored. Since,
therefore, the substance of the mind has been found to be
extraordinarily mobile, it must consist of particles exceptionally small and smooth and round. This discovery, my
dear fellow, will prove a timely aid to you in many problems.

Here is a further indication how flimsy is the texture of
the vital spirit and in how small a space it could be contained if it could be massed together. At the instant when a
man is mastered by the care-free calm of death and forsaken
by mind and spirit, you cannot tell either by sight or by
weight that any part of the whole has been filched away
from his body. Death leaves everything there, except vital
sentience and warmth. Therefore the vital spirit as a whole
must consist of very tiny atoms, linked together throughout
veins, flesh and sinews – atoms so small that, when all the
spirit has escaped from the whole body, the outermost
contour of the limbs appears intact and there is no loss of
weight. The same thing happens when the bouquet has
evaporated from the juice of Bacchus, or the sweet perfume
of an ointment has escaped into the air, or some substance
has lost its savour. The substance itself is not visibly
diminished by the loss, and its weight is not lessened,
obviously because savour and scent are caused by many

minute atoms distributed throughout the mass. On every ground, therefore, it may be inferred that mind and spirit are composed of exceptionally diminutive atoms, since their departure is not accompanied by any loss of weight.

It must not be supposed that the stuff of mind or spirit is a single element. The body at death is abandoned by a sort of rarefied wind mixed with warmth, while the warmth carries with it also air. Indeed, heat never occurs without an intermixture of air: because it is naturally sparse, it must have many atoms of air moving in its interstices.

The composition of mind is thus found to be *at least three-fold*. But all these three components together are not enough to create sentience, since the mind does not admit that any of these can create the sensory motions that originate the meditations revolved in the mind. *We must* accordingly *add to these a fourth component*, which is quite nameless. Than this there is nothing more mobile or more tenuous – nothing whose component atoms are smaller or smoother. This it is that first sets the sensory motions coursing through the limbs. Owing to the minuteness of its atoms, it is first to be stirred. Then the motions are caught up by warmth and the unseen energy of wind, then by air. Then everything is roused to movement: the blood is quickened; the impulse spreads throughout the flesh; last of all, bones and marrow are thrilled with pleasure or the opposite excitement. To this extremity pain cannot lightly penetrate, or the pangs of anguish win through. If they do, then everything is so confounded that no room is left for life, and the components of the vital spirit escape through all the pores of the body. But usually a stop is put to these movements as near as may be at the surface of the body. Thanks to this stoppage we contrive to cling on to life.

At this point I should like to demonstrate *how these components are intermixed* and from what mode of combination they derive their powers. Reluctantly I am thwarted in my purpose by the poverty of our native tongue. But, so far as I can touch upon the surface of this topic, I will tackle it.

The atoms rush in and out amongst one another on atomic trajectories, so that no one of them can be segregated nor its distinctive power isolated by intervening space. They co-exist like the many properties of a single body. In the flesh of any living thing there are regularly scent and colour and taste; and yet from all these there is formed only one corporeal bulk. Just so, warmth and air and the unseen energy of wind create in combination a single substance, together with that mobile force which imparts to them from itself the initial impetus from which the sensory motion takes its rise throughout the flesh. This basic substance lurks at our very core. There is nothing in our bodies more fundamental than this, the most vital element of their whole vital spirit. Just as in our limbs and body as a whole mind and spirit with their interconnected powers are latent, because their component atoms are small and sparse, so this nameless element composed of minute atoms is latent in the vital spirit and is in turn its vital element and controls the whole body.

In the same way, wind and air and warmth commingled through the limbs must interact, one being relatively latent, another prominent. In appearance a single stuff is formed by them all: warmth and wind and air do not display their powers separately so as to blot out sentience and dissolve it by their disunion. First, there is at the mind's disposal that element of heat which it brings into play when it boils with rage and passion blazes more fiercely from the eyes. There is likewise no lack of that chill wind, associated with fear, which sets the limbs atremble and impels them to flight. There is lastly that calm and steady air which prevails in a tranquil breast and unruffled mien.

In those creatures whose passionate hearts and choleric dispositions easily boil up in anger, there is a surplus of the hot element. An outstanding example is the truculent temper of lions, who often roar till they burst their chests with bellowing and cannot keep the torrents of their rage pent within. But the cold hearts of deer are of a windier blend: they are quicker to set chill breezes blowing through the flesh, provoking a shuddering movement in the limbs. Cattle, again, have in their vital composition a bigger portion of calm air. They are never too hotly fired by a touch of that smoky torch of anger which clouds the mind with its black and blinding shadow. They are never transfixed and benumbed by the icy shaft of fear. Their nature is a mean between the timidity of the deer and the lion's ferocity.

So it is with men. Though education may apply a similar polish to various individuals, it still leaves fundamental traces of their several temperaments. It must not be supposed that innate vices can be completely eradicated: one man will still incline more readily to outbursts of rage; another will give way a little sooner to fear; a third will accept some contingencies too impassively. And in a host of other ways men must differ one from another in temperament and so also in the resultant behaviour. To unfold here the secret causes of these differences is beyond my power. I cannot even find names for the multiplicity of atomic shapes that give rise to this variety of types. But I am clear that there is one relevant fact I can affirm: the lingering traces of inborn temperament that cannot be eliminated by

philosophy are so slight that there is nothing to prevent
men from leading a life worthy of the gods.

This *vital spirit*, then, *is present in the whole body*. It is the
body's guardian and preserver. For the two are interlocked
by common roots and cannot be torn apart without manifest
disaster. As easily could the scent be torn out of lumps of
incense without destroying their nature as mind and spirit
could be abstracted from the whole body without total
dissolution. So from their earliest origin the two are charged
with a communal life by the intertangled atoms that compose them. It is clear that neither body nor mind by itself
without the other's aid possesses the power of sensation: it
is by the interacting motions of the two combined that the
flame of sentience is kindled in our flesh.

Again, body by itself never experiences birth or growth,
and we see that it does not persist after death. Water, we
know, often gives up the heat imparted to it without being
disrupted in the process, and survives intact. Not so can the
derelict limbs outlast the departure of the vital spirit: they
are utterly demolished by internal decomposition and
decay. So from the very beginning, even when they are at
rest in the mother's womb, body and spirit in mutual
contact acquire the motions that generate life. They cannot
be wrenched apart without hurt and havoc. So you may see,
since their very existence depends upon conjunction, that
their nature must likewise be conjoint.

If anyone still denies that the body is sentient, and
believes it is the spirit interfused throughout the body that
assumes this motion which we term sensation, he is fighting
against manifest facts. Who can explain what bodily sensation really is, if it is not such as it is palpably presented to
us by experience? Admittedly, when the spirit is banished,

the body is quite insensible. That is because what it loses was never one of its permanent properties, but one of many attributes which it loses at death.

Again, it is awkward to maintain that the eyes can see nothing, but the mind peeps out through them as though through open doors. The sense of sight itself leads us the other way, dragging and tugging us right to the eyeballs. Often, for instance, we cannot see bright objects, because our eyes are dazzled by light. This is an experience unknown to doors: the doorways through which we gaze suffer no distress by being flung open. Besides, if our eyes are equivalent to doors, then when the eyes are removed the mind obviously ought to see things better now that the doors are away, doorposts and all.

Another error to be avoided, and one that is sanctioned by the revered authority of the great Democritus, is the belief that the limbs are knit together by atoms of body and mind arranged alternately, first one and then the other. In fact, *the atoms of spirit are not only much less in magnitude than those composing our body and flesh; they are also correspondingly inferior in number* and scattered but sparsely through our limbs. Observe what are the smallest objects whose impact serves to excite sensory motions in our bodies: these will give you the measure of the gaps between the atoms of spirit. Sometimes we are unaware that dust is sticking to our bodies or a cloud of chalk has settled on our limbs; we do not feel the night mist, or the slight threads of gossamer in our path that enmesh us as we walk, or the fall of a flimsy cobweb on our heads, or plumes of birds or flying thistledown, which from their very lightness do not lightly descend. We do not mark the path of every creeping thing that crawls across our body or every separate footfall planted by a gnat or midge. So quite a considerable commotion must be made in our bodies before the atomic disturbance is felt by the atoms of spirit interspersed through our limbs and before these can knock together across the intervening gaps and clash and combine and again bounce apart.

Note also that *it is mind, far more than spirit, that keeps life under lock and key* – mind that has the greater mastery over life. Without mind and intellect no scrap of vital spirit can linger one instant in our limbs. Spirit follows smoothly in the wake of mind and scatters into the air, leaving the limbs cold with the chill of death. While mind remains, life remains. One whose limbs are all lopped from the mangled trunk, despite the loss of vital spirit released from the limbs, yet lives and inhales the life-giving gusts of air. Though robbed, if not of all, at least of a large proportion of his spirit, he lingers still in life and clings fast to it. Just so, though the eye is lacerated all round, so long as the pupil remains intact, the faculty of vision remains alive, provided always that you do not hack away the whole encircling orb and leave the eyeball detached and isolated; for that cannot be done without total destruction. But tamper with that tiny bit in the middle of the eye, and out goes the light there and then and darkness falls, although the shining orb is otherwise unscathed. It is on just such terms that spirit and mind are everlastingly linked together.

My next point is this: you must understand that the *minds of living things and the light fabric of their spirits are neither birthless nor deathless*. To this end I have long been mustering and inventing verses with a labour that is also a joy. Now I will try to set them out in a style worthy of your career.

Please note that both objects are to be embraced under one name. When, for instance, I proceed to demonstrate that 'spirit' is mortal, you must understand that this applies equally to 'mind', since the two are so conjoined as to constitute a single substance.

First of all, then, I have shown that spirit is flimsy stuff composed of tiny particles. Its atoms are obviously far smaller than those of swift-flowing water or mist or smoke, since it far outstrips them in mobility and is moved by a far slighter impetus. Indeed, it is actually moved by images of smoke and mist. So, for instance, when we are sunk in sleep, we may see altars sending up clouds of steam and giving off smoke; and we cannot doubt that we are here dealing with images. Now, we see that water flows out in all directions from a broken vessel and the moisture is dissipated, and mist and smoke vanish into thin air. Be assured, therefore, that spirit is similarly dispelled and vanishes far more speedily and is sooner dissolved into its component atoms once it has been let loose from the human frame. When the body, which served as a vessel for it, is by some means broken and attenuated by loss of blood from the veins, so as to be no longer able to contain it, how can you suppose that it can be contained by any kind of air, which must be far more tenuous than our bodily frame?

Again, we are conscious that mind and body are born together, grow up together and together decay. With the weak and delicate frame of wavering childhood goes a like infirmity of judgement. The robust vigour of ripening years is accompanied by a steadier resolve and a maturer strength of mind. Later, when the body is palsied by the potent forces of age and the limbs begin to droop with blunted

vigour, the understanding limps, the tongue falters and the
mind totters: everything weakens and gives way at the same
time. It is thus natural that the vital spirit should all
evaporate like smoke, soaring into the gusty air, since we
have seen that it shares the body's birth and growth and
wearies with the weariness of age.

Furthermore, as the body suffers the horrors of disease
and the pangs of pain, so we see the mind stabbed with
anguish, grief and fear. What more natural than that it
should likewise have a share in death? Often enough in the
body's illness the mind wanders. It raves and babbles dis-
tractedly. At times it drifts on a tide of drowsiness, with
drooping eyelids and nodding head, into a deep and endless
sleep, from which it cannot hear the voices or recognize the
faces of those who stand around with streaming eyes and
tear-stained cheeks, striving to recall it to life. Since the
mind is thus invaded by the contagion of disease, you must
acknowledge that it is destructible. For pain and sickness
are the artificers of death, as we have been taught by the
fate of many men before us.

Again, when the pervasive power of wine has entered into
a man and its glow is dispersed through his veins, his limbs
are overcome by heaviness; his legs stagger and stumble;
his speech is slurred, his mind besotted; his eyes swim;
there is a crescendo of shouts, hiccups, oaths; and all the
other symptoms follow in due order. Why should this be,
if not because the wanton wildness of the wine has power
to dislodge the vital spirit within the body? And, when
things can be dislodged and arrested, this is an indication
that the inroad of a slightly more potent force would make
an end of them and rob them of a future.

Or it may happen that a man is seized with a sudden
spasm of epilepsy before our eyes. He falls as though struck

by lightning and foams at the mouth. He groans and trembles in every joint. He raves. He contracts his muscles. He writhes. He gasps convulsively. He tires his limbs with tossing. The cause of the foaming is that the force of the disease, dispersed through the limbs, dislodges the vital spirit and lashes it to spray, as the wild wind's fury froths the salt sea waves. The groans are wrung from him because his limbs are racked with pain and in general because atoms of vocal sound are expelled and whirled out in a lump through the mouth – their customary outlet, where the way is already paved for them. The raving occurs because mind and spirit are dislodged and, as I have explained, split up and scattered this way and that by the same toxin. Then, when the cause of the disease has passed its climax and the morbid secretion of the distempered body ebbs back to its secret abode, then the man rises, swaying unsteadily at first, and returns bit by bit to all his senses and recovers his vital spirit. When mind and spirit in the body itself are a prey to such violent maladies and suffer such distressing dispersal, how can you believe them capable of surviving apart from the body in the open air with the wild winds for company?

Conversely, we see that the mind, like a sick body, can be healed and directed by medicine. This too is a presage that its life is mortal. When you embark on an attempt to alter the mind or to direct any other natural object, it is fair to suppose that you are adding certain parts or transposing them or subtracting some trifle at any rate from their sum. But an immortal object will not let its parts be rearranged or added to, or the least bit drop off. For, if ever anything is so transformed as to overstep its own limits, this means the immediate death of what was before. By this susceptibility both to sickness (as I have shown) and to medicine, the mind displays the marks of mortality. So false reasoning is plainly confronted by true fact. Every loophole is barred to its exponent, and by the two horns of a dilemma he is convicted of falsehood.

Again, we often see a man pass away little by little, and lose his vital sensibility limb by limb: first the toes and toe-nails lose their colour; then the feet and legs die; after that the imprint of icy death steals by slow degrees through the other members. Since the vital spirit is thus dispersed and does not come out all at once in its entirety, it must be regarded as mortal. You may be tempted to suppose that it can shrink into itself through the body and draw its parts together and so withdraw sensibility from every limb. But, if that were so, the place in which such a mass of spirit was concentrated ought to display an exceptional degree of sensibility. Since there is no such place, it evidently leaks out in driblets, as I said before – in other words, it perishes. Let us, however, concede this false hypothesis and suppose that the spirit concentrates within the body of those who leave the light of day through a creeping palsy. You must still acknowledge that spirit is mortal. It makes no odds whether it is scattered to the winds and disintegrated, or concentrated and deadened. In either case, the victim as a whole is more and more drained of sensibility in every part, and in every part less and less of life remains.

The mind, again, is a part of a man and stays fixed in a particular spot, no less than the ears and eyes and other senses by which life is guided. Now, our hand or eye or nostrils in isolation from us cannot experience sensation or even exist; in a very short time they rot away. So mind cannot exist apart from body and from the man himself who is, as it were, a vessel for it – or if you choose you may picture it as something still more intimately linked, since body clings to mind by close ties.

Again, mind and body as a living force derive their vigour and vitality from their conjunction. Without body, the mind alone cannot perform the vital motions. Bereft of vital spirit, the body cannot persist and exercise its senses. As the eye uprooted and separated from the body cannot see, so we perceive that spirit and mind by themselves are powerless. It is only because their atoms are held in by the whole body, intermingled through veins and flesh, sinews and bones, and are not free to bounce far apart, that they are kept together so as to perform the motions that generate sentience. After death, when they are expelled out of the body into the gusty air, they cannot perform the sensory motions because they are no longer held together in the same way. The air indeed will itself be a body, and an animate one at that, if it allows the vital spirit to hang together and keep up those motions which it used to go through before in the sinews and the body itself. Here then is proof upon proof. You must perforce admit that, when the whole bodily envelope crumbles after the expulsion of the vital breath, the senses of the mind and the spirit likewise disintegrate, since body and mind are effects of the same cause.

Again, the body cannot suffer the withdrawal of the vital spirit without rotting away in a foul stench. How can you doubt, then, but that the spirit diffused in the depths of the body has come to the surface and evaporated like smoke? That explains why the body is transformed and collapses so utterly into decay: its inmost foundations are sapped by the effusion of the spirit through the limbs and through all the body's winding channels and chinks. So there are many indications that the vital spirit seeps out through the limbs in driblets and is already split up within the body before it slips out and glides into the gusty air.

No one on the point of death seems to feel his spirit retiring intact right out of his body or rising first to his gullet and up through his throat. On the contrary, he feels that it is failing in a particular region which it occupies, just as he is conscious that his other senses are being extinguished each in its own sphere. If our mind were indeed immortal, it would not complain of extinction in the hour of death, but would feel rather that it was escaping from confinement and sloughing off its garment like a snake.

Even while the vital spirit yet lingers within the boundaries of life, it often seems, when something has violently upset it, as though it were struggling to escape and be wholly released from the body – as though the features were relaxing into their ultimate immobility and every limb were ready to hang limp upon the bloodless trunk. It is at such times that we say 'the mind has had a shock' or 'the spirit has fled'. The fear of death is already upon us, and everyone is straining to hold fast the last link with life. Then the mind and all the vital spirit are churned up and both these, together with the body, are on the point of collapse, so that a slightly intensified force might shatter them. How can you doubt, then, that the fragile spirit once stripped of its envelope and thrust out of the body into the open would be powerless not only to survive throughout eternity but even to persist for a single instant?

Again, why is mind or thought never born in head or feet or hands? Why does it cling fast in every man to one spot or a specified region? It can only be that a specific place is assigned to each thing where it can be born and survive. So every creature is created with a great diversity of members, whose mutual position is never reversed. One thing duly follows another: flame is not born in a flood, nor frost begotten in fire.

Moreover, if the spirit is by nature immortal and can remain sentient when divorced from our body, we must credit it, I presume, with the possession of five senses. In no other way can we picture to ourselves departed spirits wandering through the Infernal Regions. So it is that painters and bygone generations of writers have portrayed spirits in possession of their senses. But eyes or nostrils or hand or tongue or ears cannot be attached to a disembodied spirit. Such a spirit cannot therefore be sentient or so much as exist.

We feel that vital sentience resides in the body as a whole and we see that the whole body is animate. Suppose, then, that it is suddenly sliced through the middle by some swiftly delivered slash, so as to fall into two quite separate parts. Without doubt the vital spirit will also be severed and split in two along with the body. But what is cleft and falls apart obviously resigns all pretensions that its nature is immortal. They say that in the heat and indiscriminate carnage of battle limbs are often lopped off by scythe-armed chariots so suddenly that the fallen member hewn from the body is seen to writhe on the ground. Yet the mind and consciousness of the man cannot yet feel the pain: so abrupt is the hurt, and so intent the mind upon the business of battle. With what is left of his body he presses on with battle and bloodshed unaware, it may be, that his left arm together with its shield has been lost, whirled away among the chargers by the chariot wheels with their predatory blades. Another does not notice that his right arm has gone, while he scrambles and struggles. Another, who has lost a leg, does his best to stand up, while on the ground at his side the dying foot twitches its toes. A head hewn from the still warm and living trunk retains on the ground its lively features and open eyes till it has yielded

up the last shred of spirit. Or take for example a snake with
flickering tongue, menacing tail and protracted body.
Should you choose to hack it in many pieces with a blade,
you will see, while the wound is fresh, every severed
portion separately squirming and spattering the ground
with gore, and the foremost part twisting back with its
mouth to bite itself in the fierce agony of the wound.
Shall we say that in each of these parts there is an entire
spirit? But on that hypothesis it would follow that one
animate creature had in its body many spirits. Actually, a
spirit that was one has been split up along with the body.
So both alike must be reckoned mortal, since both alike
are split into many parts.

Next, if the spirit is by nature immortal and is slipped
into the body at birth, why do we retain no memory of
an earlier existence, no impress of antecedent events? If
the mind's operation is so greatly changed that all record of
former actions has been expunged, it is no long journey, in
my judgement, from this experience to annihilation. So you
must admit that the pre-existent spirit has died and the one
that is now is a new creation.

Let us suppose, for argument's sake, that the vital force
of mind is introduced into us when the body is already fully
formed, at the moment when we are born and step across
the threshold of life. This theory does not square with the
observed fact that the mind grows with the bodily frame
and in the very blood. It would imply that the mind lived
in solitary confinement, alone in its cell, and yet at the
same time the whole body was shot through with sentience.
Here then is proof upon proof that spirits are not to be
regarded as birthless, nor yet as exempt from the law of
death. If they were slipped into our bodies from outside, it
cannot be supposed that the two would be so closely inter-

locked as they are shown to be by the clearest evidence.
For spirit so interpenetrates veins, flesh, sinews, bones,
that our very teeth share in sensation – witness toothache
and the shock of contact with icy water or a jagged stone
buried in a loaf. Being thus interwoven, it does not seem
possible that it should escape intact and extricate itself
undamaged from every sinew, bone and joint. Or, if you
suppose that, after being slipped in from outside, the spirit
oozes through our limbs, then it is all the more bound to
perish with the body through which it is thus interfused.
To ooze through something is to be dissolved in it and
therefore to perish. We know that food, when it is rationed
out amongst our limbs and members by diffusion through
all the channels of the body, is destroyed and takes on a
different nature. Just so, on the assumption that spirit and
mind enter into the newly formed body as complete entities,
they must be dissolved in oozing through it : our limbs must
be interpenetrated through every channel by the particles
composing this mind which lords it now in our body – this
new mind born of the old one that must have perished in
its diffusion through our limbs. It is thus evident that the
human spirit is neither independent of a birthday nor
immune from a latter end.

The further question arises whether or not any atoms of
vital spirit are left in a lifeless body. If some are left and
lodge there, we are not justified in regarding the spirit as
immortal, since it has come away mutilated by the loss of
some of its parts. If, on the other hand, it withdraws with
its members intact, so that no scrap of it remains in the
body, how is it that corpses, when their flesh begins to rot,
exude maggots? What is the source of that boneless and
bloodless horde of animate things that swarms through the
swollen limbs? You may argue that spirits can slip into the

maggots from outside and settle individually in their bodies. I will not ask why in that case many thousands of spirits should forgather in the place from which one has withdrawn. But there is another question that calls for a decisive answer. Do these supposed spirits each hunt out atoms of maggots and manufacture dwelling-places for themselves? Or do they slip into ready-made bodies? No adequate reason can be given why they should undertake the labour of manufacture. In their bodiless state they presumably flit about untroubled by sickness, cold or hunger. For the body is far more subject to these afflictions, and communion with it is the source of many of the mind's troubles. But suppose they had the best of reasons for making a body to which they could subject themselves: there is no discernible way in which they could set about it. So much for the suggestion that spirits make bodies and limbs for themselves. We may equally rule out the alternative theory that they slip into ready-made bodies. For this would not account for the intimate communion between body and spirit and their sensory interaction.

Again, why is grim ferocity an attribute of the lions' surly breed, as craftiness of foxes? Why are deer endowed by their parents with timidity and their limbs impelled to flight by hereditary tremors? Why are all other traits of this sort implanted in physique and character from birth? It can only be because the mind always shares in the specific growth of the body according to its seed and breed. If it were immortal and passed from body to body, there would be living things of jumbled characters. Often the hound of Hyrcanian breed would turn tail before the onset of the antlered stag. The hawk would flee trembling through the gusty air at the coming of the dove. Man would be witless, and brute beasts rational. It is an untenable theory that an immortal spirit is modified by a change of body. For whatever changes is disintegrated and therefore destroyed. The component parts of spirits are in any case transposed and reshuffled. So the spirits as a whole might just as well be diffused through the limbs and eventually destroyed with the body. If, on the other hand, it is maintained that the spirits of men enter none but human bodies, then I would ask why a wise one should become foolish – why a child is never rational, nor a mare's foal as accomplished as a sturdy steed. The one loophole left is the assumption that in a frail body the mind too grows frail. But in that case you must admit that the spirit is mortal, since in its adaptation to the bodily frame it loses so utterly its previous vitality and sensibility. How can the mind wax stronger in unison with each particular body till it attains with it the coveted season of full bloom, unless the two are coheirs of a single birth? Why, when the limbs are wasted with age, should the mind wish to slip out and away? Is it afraid to stay locked up in a mouldering body? Afraid that its lodging may collapse from the wear and tear of age? Surely an immortal being need fear no danger.

Again, it is surely ludicrous to suppose that spirits are standing by at the mating and birth of animals – a numberless number of immortals on the look-out for mortal frames, jostling and squabbling to get in first and establish themselves most firmly. Or is there perhaps an established compact that first come shall be first served, without any trial of strength between spirit and spirit?

A tree cannot exist high in air, or clouds in the depths of the sea, as fish cannot live in the fields, or blood flow in wood or sap in stones. There is a determined and allotted place for the growth and presence of everything. So mind cannot arise alone without body or apart from sinews and blood. If it could do this, then surely it could much more readily function in head or shoulders or the tips of the heels and be born in any other part, so long as it was held in the same container, that is to say in the same man. Since, however, even in the human body we see a determined and allotted place set aside for the growth and presence of spirit and mind, we have even stronger grounds for denying that they could survive or come to birth outside the body altogether. You must admit, therefore, that when the body has perished there is an end also of the spirit diffused through it. It is surely crazy to couple a mortal object with an eternal and suppose that they can work in harmony and mutually interact. What can be imagined more incongruous, what more repugnant and discordant, than that a mortal object and one that is immortal and everlasting should unite to form a compound and jointly weather the storms that rage about them?

Again, there can be only three kinds of everlasting objects. The first, owing to the absolute solidity of their substance, can repel blows and let nothing penetrate them so as to unknit their close texture from within. Such are the atoms of matter, whose nature I have already demonstrated. The second kind can last for ever because it is immune from blows. Such is empty space, which remains untouched and unaffected by any impact. Last is that which has no available place surrounding it into which its matter can disperse and disintegrate. It is for this reason that the sum total of the universe is everlasting, having no space outside it into which the matter can escape and no matter that can enter and disintegrate it by the force of impact.

Equally vain is the suggestion that the spirit is immortal because it is shielded by life-preserving powers; or because it is unassailed by forces hostile to its survival; or because such forces, if they threaten, are somehow arrested before we are conscious of the threat. Apart from the spirit's participation in the ailments of the body, it has maladies enough of its own. The prospect of the future torments it with fear and wearies it with worry, and past misdeeds leave the sting of remorse. Lastly, it may fall a prey to the mind's own specific afflictions, madness and amnesia, and plunge into the black waters of oblivion.

From all this it follows that *death is nothing to us* and no concern of ours, since our tenure of the mind is mortal. In days of old, we felt no disquiet when the hosts of Carthage poured in to battle on every side – when the whole earth, dizzied by the convulsive shock of war, reeled sickeningly under the high ethereal vault, and between realm and realm the empire of mankind by land and sea trembled in the balance. So, when we shall be no more – when the union of body and spirit that engenders us has been disrupted – to us, who shall then be nothing, nothing by any hazard will happen any more at all. Nothing will have power to stir our senses, not though earth be fused with sea and sea with sky.

If any feeling remains in mind or spirit after it has been torn from our body, that is nothing to us, who are brought into being by the wedlock of body and spirit, conjoined and coalesced. Or even if the matter that composes us should be reassembled by time after our death and brought back into its present state – if the light of life were given to us anew – even that contingency would still be no concern of ours once the chain of our identity had been snapped. We who are now are not concerned with ourselves in any previous existence: the sufferings of those selves do not touch us. When you look at the immeasurable extent of time gone by and the multiform movements of matter, you will readily credit that these same atoms that compose us now must many a time before have entered into the self-same combinations as now. But our mind cannot recall this to remembrance. For between then and now is interposed a breach in life, and all the atomic motions have been wandering far astray from sentience.

If the future holds travail and anguish in store, the self must be in existence, when that time comes, in order to experience it. But from this fate we are redeemed by death, which denies existence to the self that might have suffered these tribulations. Rest assured, therefore, that we have nothing to fear in death. One who no longer is cannot suffer, or differ in any way from one who has never been born, when once this mortal life has been usurped by death the immortal.

When you find a man treating it as a grievance that after death he will either moulder in the grave or fall a prey to flames or to the jaws of predatory beasts, be sure that his utterance does not ring true. Subconsciously his heart is stabbed by a secret dread, however loudly the man himself may disavow the belief that after death he will still experience sensation. I am convinced that he does not grant the admission he professes, nor the grounds of it; he does not oust and pluck himself root and branch out of life, but all unwittingly makes something of himself linger on. When a living man confronts the thought that after death his body will be mauled by birds and beasts of prey, he is filled with self-pity. He does not banish himself from the scene nor distinguish sharply enough between himself and that abandoned carcass. He visualizes that object as himself and infects it with his own feelings as an onlooker. That is why he is aggrieved at having been created mortal. He does not

see that in real death there will be no other self alive to
mourn his own decease – no other self standing by to flinch
at the agony he suffers lying there being mangled, or indeed
being cremated. For if it is really a bad thing after death to
be mauled and crunched by ravening jaws, I cannot see why
it should not be disagreeable to roast in the scorching
flames of a funeral pyre, or to lie embalmed in honey,
stifled and stiff with cold, on the surface of a chilly slab, or
to be squashed under a crushing weight of earth.

'Now it is all over. Now the happy home and the best of
wives will welcome you no more, nor winsome children
rush to snatch the first kiss at your coming and touch your
heart with speechless joy. No chance now to further your
fortune or safeguard your family. Unhappy man,' they
cry, 'unhappily cheated by one treacherous day out of all
the uncounted blessings of life!' But they do not go on to
say: 'And now no repining for these lost joys will oppress
you any more.' If they perceived this clearly with their
minds and acted according to the words, they would free
their breasts from a great load of grief and dread.

'Ah yes! *You* are at peace now in the sleep of death, and
so you will stay to the end of time. Pain and sorrow will
never touch you again. But to *us*, who stood weeping incon-
solably while you were consumed to ashes on the dreadful
pyre – to us no day will come that will lift the undying
sorrow from our hearts.' Ask the speaker, then, what is so
heart-rending about this. If something returns to sleep and
peace, what reason is that for pining in inconsolable grief?

Here, again, is the way men often talk from the bottom
of their hearts when they recline at a banquet, goblet in
hand and brows decked with garlands: 'How all too short
are these good times that come to us poor creatures! Soon
they will be past and gone, and there will be no recalling

them.' You would think the crowning calamity in store for
them after death was to be parched and shrivelled by a
tormenting thirst or oppressed by some other vain desire.
But even in sleep, when mind and body alike are at rest, no
one misses himself or sighs for life. If such sleep were prolonged to eternity, no longing for ourselves would trouble
us. And yet the vital atoms in our limbs cannot be far
removed from their sensory motions at a time when a mere
jolt out of sleep enables a man to pull himself together.
Death, therefore, must be regarded, so far as we are concerned, as having much less existence than sleep, if anything
can have less existence than what we perceive to be nothing.
For death is followed by a far greater dispersal of the seething mass of matter: once that icy breach in life has inter-
vened, there is no more waking.

Suppose that Nature herself were suddenly to find a voice
and round upon one of us in these terms: 'What is your
grievance, mortal, that you give yourself up to this whining
and repining? Why do you weep and wail over death? If the
life you have lived till now has been a pleasant thing – if all
its blessings have not leaked away like water poured into a
cracked pot and run to waste unrelished – why then, you
silly creature, do you not retire as a guest who has had his
fill of life and take your care-free rest with a quiet mind?
Or, if all your gains have been poured profitless away and
life has grown distasteful, why do you seek to swell the
total? The new can but turn out as badly as the old and
perish as unprofitably. Why not rather make an end of life
and labour? Do you expect me to invent some new contrivance for your pleasure? I tell you, there is none. All things
are always same. If your body is not yet withered with
age, nor your limbs decrepit and flagging, even so there is
nothing new to look forward to – not though you should

outlive all living creatures, or even though you should never die at all.' What are we to answer, except that Nature's rebuttal is justified and the plea she puts forward is a true one?

But suppose it is some man of riper years who complains – some dismal greybeard who frets unconscionably at his approaching end. Would she not have every right to protest more vehemently and repulse him in stern tones: 'Away with your tears, old reprobate! Have done with your grumbling! You are withering now after tasting all the joys of life. But, because you are always pining for what is not and unappreciative of the things at hand, your life has slipped away unfulfilled and unprized. Death has stolen upon you unawares, before you are ready to retire from life's banquet filled and satisfied. Come now, put away all that is unbecoming to your years and compose your mind to make way for others. You have no choice.' I cannot question but she would have right on her side; her censure and rebuke would be well merited. The old is always thrust aside to make way for the new, and one thing must be built out of the wreck of another. There is no murky pit of Hell awaiting anyone. There is need of matter, so that later generations may arise; when they have lived out their span, they will all follow you. Bygone generations have taken your road, and those to come will take it no less. So one thing will never cease to spring from another. To none is life given in freehold; to all on lease. Look back at the eternity that passed before we were born, and mark how utterly it counts to us as nothing. This is a mirror that Nature holds up to us, in which we may see the time that shall be after we are dead. Is there anything terrifying in the sight – anything depressing – anything that is not more restful than the soundest sleep?

As for all those torments that are said to take place in the depths of Hell, they are actually present here and now, in our own lives.

There is no wretched Tantalus, as the myth relates, transfixed with groundless terror at the huge boulder poised above him in the air. But in this life there really are mortals oppressed by unfounded fear of the gods and trembling at the impending doom that may fall upon any of them at the whim of chance.

There is no Tityos lying in Hell for ever probed by birds of prey. Assuredly they cannot find food by groping under those giant ribs to glut them throughout eternity. No matter to what length that titanic frame may lie outstretched, so that he covers not a paltry nine acres with his spread-eagled limbs but the whole extent of earth, he will not be able to suffer an eternity of pain nor furnish food from his body for evermore. But Tityos is here in our midst – that poor devil prostrated by love, torn indeed by birds of prey, devoured by gnawing jealousy or rent by the fangs of some other passion.

Sisyphus too is alive for all to see, bent on winning the insignia of office, its rods and ruthless axes, by the people's vote and embittered by perpetual defeat. To strive for this profitless and never-granted prize, and in striving toil and moil incessantly, this truly is to push a boulder laboriously up a steep hill, only to see it, once the top is reached, rolling and bounding down again to the flat levels of the plain.

By the same token, to be for ever feeding a malcontent mind, filling it with good things but never satisfying it – the fate we suffer when the circling seasons enrich us with their products and their ever-changing charms but we are never filled with the fruits of life – this surely exemplifies the story of those maidens in the flower of life for ever pouring water into a leaking vessel which can never by any sleight be filled.

As for Cerberus and the Furies and the pitchy darkness and the jaws of Hell belching abominable fumes, these are not and cannot be anywhere at all. But life is darkened by the fear of retribution for our misdeeds, a fear enormous in proportion to their enormity, and by the penalties imposed for crime – imprisonment and ghastly precipitation from Tarpeia's Crag, the lash, the block, the rack, the boiling pitch, the firebrand and the branding iron. Even though these horrors are not physically present, yet the conscience-ridden mind in terrified anticipation torments itself with its own goads and whips. It does not see what term there can be to its suffering nor where its punishment can have an end. It is afraid that death may serve merely to intensify pain. So at length the life of misguided mortals becomes a Hell on earth.

Here is something that you might well say to yourself from time to time: 'Even good king Ancus looked his last on the daylight – a better man than you, my presumptuous friend, by a long reckoning. Death has come to many another monarch and potentate, who lorded it over mighty nations. Even that King of Kings who once built a highway across the great deep – who gave his legions a path to tread among the waves and taught them to march on foot over the briny gulfs and with his chargers trampled scornfully upon the ocean's roar – even he was robbed of the light and poured out the spirit from a dying frame. Scipio, that thunderbolt of war, the terror of Carthage, gave his bones to the earth as if he had been the meanest of serfs. Add to this company the discoverers of truth and beauty. Add the attendants of the Muses, among them Homer who in solitary glory bore

the sceptre but has sunk into the same slumber as the rest.
Democritus, when ripe age warned him that the mindful
motions of his intellect were running down, made his
unbowed head a willing sacrifice to death. And the Master
himself, when his daylit race was run, Epicurus himself died,
whose genius outshone the race of men and dimmed them
all, as the stars are dimmed by the rising of the fiery sun.
And will *you* kick and protest against your sentence? You,
whose life is next-door to death while you are still alive and
looking on the light. You, who waste the major part of your
time in sleep and, when you are awake, are snoring still
and dreaming. You, who bear a mind hag-ridden by baseless
fear and cannot find the commonest cause of your distress,
hounded as you are, poor creature, by a pack of troubles and
drifting in a drunken stupor upon a wavering tide of
fantasy.'

Men feel plainly enough within their minds, a heavy
burden, whose weight depresses them. If only they perceived with equal clearness the causes of this depression,
the origin of this lump of evil within their breasts, they
would not lead such a life as we now see all too commonly –
no one knowing what he really wants and everyone for ever
trying to get away from where he is, as though mere loco-
motion could throw off the load. Often the owner of some
stately mansion, bored stiff by staying at home, takes his
departure, only to return as speedily when he feels himself
no better off out of doors. Off he goes to his country seat,
driving his carriage and pair hot-foot, as though in haste to
save a house on fire. No sooner has he crossed its doorstep
than he starts yawning or retires moodily to sleep and courts
oblivion, or else rushes back to revisit the city. In so doing
the individual is really running away from himself. Since he
remains reluctantly wedded to the self whom he cannot of

course escape, he grows to hate him, because he is a sick man ignorant of the cause of his malady. If he did but see this, he would cast other thoughts aside and devote himself first to studying the nature of the universe. It is not the fortune of an hour that is in question, but of all time – the lot in store for mortals throughout the eternity that awaits them after death.

What is this deplorable lust of life that holds us trembling in bondage to such uncertainties and dangers? A fixed term is set to the life of mortals, and there is no way of dodging death. In any case the setting of our lives remains the same throughout, and by going on living we do not mint any new coin of pleasure. So long as the object of our craving is unattained, it seems more precious than anything besides. Once it is ours, we crave for something else. So an unquenchable thirst for life keeps us always on the gasp. There is no telling what fortune the future may bring – what chance may throw in our way, or what upshot lies in waiting. By prolonging life, we cannot subtract or whittle away one jot from the duration of our death. The time after our taking off remains constant. However many generations you may add to your store by living, there waits for you none the less the same eternal death. The time of not-being will be no less for him who made an end of life with yesterday's daylight than for him who perished many a moon and many a year before.

Book IV

SENSATION AND SEX

*

I AM blazing a trail through pathless tracts of the Muses'
Pierian realm, where no foot has ever trod before. What
joy it is to light upon virgin springs and drink their waters.
What joy to pluck new flowers and gather for my brow a
glorious garland from fields whose blossoms were never yet
wreathed by the Muses round any head. This is my reward
for teaching on these lofty topics, for struggling to loose
men's minds from the tight knots of superstition and shedding on dark corners the bright beam of my song that
irradiates everything with the sparkle of the Muses. My art
is not without a purpose. Physicians, when they wish to
treat children with a nasty dose of wormwood, first smear
the rim of the cup with a coat of yellow honey. The children, too young as yet for foresight, are lured by the sweetness at their lips into swallowing the bitter draught. So they
are tricked but not trapped; for the treatment restores them
to health. In the same way our doctrine often seems unpalatable to those who have not sampled it, and the multitude
shrink from it. That is why I have tried to administer it to
you in the dulcet strains of poesy, coated with the sweet
honey of the Muses. My object has been to engage your
mind with my verses while you gain insight into the nature
of the universe and learn to appreciate the profit you are
reaping.

I have already shown what the component bodies of everything are like; how they vary in shape; how they fly spontaneously through space, impelled by a perpetual motion;
and how from these all objects can be created. I have
further shown what is the nature of the mind; by what
forces it is brought to its full strength in union with the
body; and how it is disintegrated and returns to its component atoms.

Now I will embark on an explanation of a highly relevant
fact, *the existence of what we call 'images' of things*, a sort of
outer skin perpetually peeled off the surface of objects and
flying about this way and that through the air. It is these
whose impact scares our minds, whether waking or sleep-
ing, on those occasions when we catch a glimpse of strange
shapes and phantoms of the dead. Often, when we are sunk
in slumber, they startle us with the notion that spirits may
get loose from Hades and ghosts hover about among the
living, and that some part of us may survive after death
when body and mind alike have been disintegrated and
dissolved into their component atoms.

I maintain therefore that replicas or insubstantial shapes
of things are thrown off from the surface of objects. These
we must denote as an outer skin or film, because each
particular floating image wears the aspect and form of
the object from whose body it has emanated. This you
may infer, however dull your wit, from the following
facts.

In the first place, within the range of vision, many
objects give off particles. Some of these are rarefied and
diffused, such as the smoke emitted by logs or the heat by
fire. Others are denser and more closely knit: cicadas, for
instance, in summer periodically shed their tubular jackets;
calves at birth cast off cauls from the surface of their

bodies; the slippery snake sloughs off on thorns the garment we often see fluttering on a briar. Since these things happen, objects must also give off a much flimsier film from the surface of their bodies. For, since those more solid emanations fall off, no reason can be given why such flimsy ones should not. Besides, we know that on the surface of objects there are lots of tiny particles, which could be thrown off without altering the order of their arrangement or the outline of their shape, and all the faster because, being relatively few and lying right on the outside, they are less liable to obstruction.

We certainly see that many objects throw off matter in abundance, not only from their inmost depths, as we have said before, but from their surfaces in the form of colour. This is done conspicuously by the awnings, yellow, scarlet and maroon, stretched flapping and billowing on poles and rafters over spacious theatres. The crowded pit below and the stage with all its scenery are made to glow and flow with the colours of the canopy. The more completely the theatre is hemmed in by surrounding walls, the more its interior, sheltered from the daylight, is irradiated by this flood of colour. Since canvasses thus give off colour from their surface, all objects must give off filmy images as a result of spraying particles from their surfaces this way and that. Here then, already definitely established, we have indications of images, flying about everywhere, extremely fine in texture and individually invisible.

Again, the reason why smell, smoke, heat and the like come streaming out of objects in shapeless clouds is that they originate in the inmost depths; so they are split up in their circuitous journey, and there are no straight vents to their channels through which they may issue directly in close formation. When the thin film of surface colour, on the other hand, is thrown off, there is nothing to disrupt it, since it lies exposed right on the outside.

Lastly, the reflections that we see in mirrors or in water or any polished surface have the same appearance as actual objects. They must therefore be composed of films given off by those objects. There exist therefore flimsy but accurate replicas of objects, individually invisible but such that, when flung back in a rapid succession of recoils from the flat surface of mirrors they produce a visible image. That is the only conceivable way in which these films can be preserved so as to reproduce such a perfect likeness of each object.

Let me now explain *how flimsy is the texture of these films*. In the first place, the atoms themselves are vastly below the range of our senses – vastly smaller than the first objects, on a descending scale, that the eye can no longer discern. In confirmation of this, let me illustrate in a few words the minuteness of the atoms of which everything is composed. First, there are animals that are already so tiny that a third part of them would be quite invisible. How are we to picture one of the internal organs of these – the tiny globule of the heart, or the eyes? Of what size are its limbs or their joints? What must be the component atoms of its spirit and its mind? You cannot help seeing how slight and diminutive these must be. Or again, consider those substances that emit a pungent odour – all-heal, bitter wormwood, oppressive southernwood, the astringent tang of centaury. If you lightly crush one of these herbs between two fingers, the scent will cling to your hand, but its particles will be quite invisible. This will convey some notion of the number of surface-films from objects that must be flying about in a variety of ways without producing any effect on the senses.

You must not suppose that the only films moving about are those that emanate from objects. *There are also films spontaneously generated* and composed in this lower region of the sky which we call the air. These assume a diversity of shapes and travel at a great height. So at times we see clouds smoothly condensing up aloft, defacing the bright aspect of the firmament and ruffling the air by their motion. Often giant faces appear to be sailing by, trailing large patches of shadow. Sometimes it seems that great mountains, or crags uprooted from mountains, are drifting by and passing over the sun. Then other clouds, black with storm, appear to be towed along in the wake of some passing monster. In their fluidity they never cease to change their form, assuming the outline now of one shape, now of another.

Let us now consider *with what facility and speed the films are generated* and ceaselessly stream out of objects and slide off their surfaces. For the outermost skin of all objects is always in readiness for them to shed. When this comes in contact with other objects, it may pass through, as it does in particular through glass. When it encounters rough rocks or solid wood, then it is promptly diffracted, so that it cannot reproduce an image. But when it is confronted by something both polished and close-grained, in particular a mirror, then neither of these things happens. The films cannot penetrate, as they do through glass; nor are they diffracted, because the smoothness ensures their preservation. That is why such surfaces reflect images that are visible to us. No matter how suddenly or at what time you set any object in front of a mirror, an image appears. From this you may infer that the surfaces of objects emit a ceaseless stream of flimsy tissues and filmy shapes. Therefore a great many films are generated in a brief space of time, so that their origin can rightly be described as instantaneous. Just as a great many particles of light must be emitted in a brief space of time by the sun to keep the world continually filled with it, so objects in general must correspondingly send off a great many images in a great many ways from every surface and in all directions instantaneously. Turn the mirror which way we will, objects are reproduced in it with corresponding shape and colour.

Again, when the weather has been most brilliant, it becomes gloomy and overcast with amazing suddenness. You would fancy that all the nether darkness from every quarter had abandoned Hades and crowded the spacious vaults of heaven: so grim a night of storm gathers aloft, from which lours down the face of black fear. In comparison with such a mass of matter, no one can express how minute a surface-film is, or convey any idea of the proportion in words.

Let me now explain in my verses *how speedily the films move* and what power they possess of swimming swiftly through the air, so that a brief hour is spent on a long journey, whatever course each one may pursue in response to its particular impulse. My account will be persuasive rather than exhaustive. Better the fleeting melody of the swan than the long-drawn clangour of cranes high up among the northward-racing clouds.

First then, it is a common observation that light objects and those composed of small particles are swift-moving. A notable example is the light and heat of the sun: these are composed of minute atoms which, when they are shoved off, lose no time in shooting right across the interspace of air in the direction imparted by the shove. The supply of light is promptly renewed by fresh light, and one flash is set going by another in a continuous procession. Similarly the films must be able to traverse an incalculable space in an instant of time, and that for two reasons. First, a very slight initial impetus far away to their rear sufficed to launch them and they continue on their course at a velocity proportionate to their lightness. Secondly, they are thrown off with such a loose-knit texture that they can readily penetrate any object and filter through the interspace of air.

Again certain particles thrown up to the surface from the inmost depths of objects, namely those that form the light and heat of the sun, are seen at the very instant of daybreak to drop and spray out across the whole space of the sky and fly over sea and lands and flood the firmament. What then of particles that are already lying right on the surface when they are thrown off and whose egress is not hampered by any obstacle? Surely they must go all the faster and the farther and traverse an extent of space many times as great in the time it takes for the sunlight to flash across the sky?

A further and especially convincing indication of the velocity of surface-films is this. Expose a smooth surface of water to the open sky when it is bright with stars: immediately the sparkling constellations of the firmament in all their unclouded splendour are reproduced in the water. Does not this indicate how instantaneous is the descent of the image from the border-land of ether to the borders of earth? Here then is proof upon proof that objects emit particles that strike upon the eyes and provoke sight.

From certain objects there also flows a perpetual stream of odour, as coolness flows from rivers, heat from the sun, and from the ocean waves a spray that eats away walls round the sea-shore. Sounds of every sort are surging incessantly through the air. When we walk by the seaside, a salty tang of brine enters our mouth; when we watch a draught of worm-wood being mixed in our presence, a bitter effluence touches it. So from every object flows a stream of matter, spreading out in all directions. The stream must flow without rest or intermission, since our senses are perpetually alert and everything is always liable to be seen or smelt or to provoke sensation by sound.

Again, when some shape or other is handled in the dark, it is recognized as the same shape that in a clear and shining light is plain to see. It follows that *touch and sight are provoked by the same stimulus.* Suppose we touch a square object and it stimulates our sense in the dark. What can it be that, given light, will strike upon our vision as square, if it is not the film emanating from the object? This shows that the cause of seeing lies in these films and without these nothing can be seen.

It is established, then, that these films, as I call them, are moving about everywhere, sprayed and scattered in all directions. Since we can see only with our eyes, we have only to direct our vision towards any particular quarter for all the objects there to strike it with their shapes and colours. Our power of perceiving and distinguishing the distance from us of each particular object is also due to the film. For, as soon as it is thrown off, it shoves and drives before it all the air that intervenes between itself and the eyes. All this air flows through our eyeballs and brushes through our pupils in passing. That is how we perceive the distance of each object: the more air is driven in front of the film and the longer the draught that brushes through our eyes, the more remote the object is seen to be. Of course this all happens so quickly that we perceive the nature of the object and its distance simultaneously.

It need occasion no surprise that, while the individual films that strike upon the eye are invisible, the objects from which they emanate are perceived. Wind too buffets us in driblets, and cold strikes us in a piercing stream; yet we do not feel each particular unit of the wind or the cold, but simply the total effect. And we see that blows are then being delivered on our body with an effect as though some external object were buffeting it and producing the sensation of its bodily presence. When we hit a stone with our toe, what we actually touch is only the outer surface of the rock, the overlying film of colour; but what we feel ourselves touching is not that but the hard inner core of the rock.

Let us now consider *why the image is seen beyond the mirror* – for it certainly does appear to be some distance behind the surface. It is just as though we were really looking out through a doorway, when the door offers a free prospect through it and affords a glimpse of many objects outside the house. In this case also the vision is accompanied by a double dose of air. First we perceive the air within the door posts; then follow the posts themselves to right and left; then the light outside and a second stretch of air brushes through the eyes, followed by the objects that are really seen out of doors. A similar thing happens when a mirrored image projects itself upon our sight. On its way to us the film shoves and drives before it all the air that intervenes between itself and the eyes, so that we feel all this before perceiving the mirror. When we have perceived the mirror itself, then the film that travels from us to it and is reflected comes back to our eyes, pushing another lot of air in front of it, so that we perceive this before the image, which thus appears to lie at some distance from the mirror. Here then is ample reason why we should not be surprised at this appearance of objects reflected in the surface of a mirror, since they involve a double journey with two lots of air.

Now for the question *why our right side appears in mirrors on the left*. The reason is that, when the film on its outward journey strikes the flat surface of a mirror, it is not slewed round intact, but flung straight back in reverse. It is just as if someone were to take a plaster mask before it had set and hurl it against a pillar or beam, so that it bounced straight back, preserving the features imprinted on its front but displaying them now in reverse. In this case what had been the right eye would now be the left and the left correspondingly would have become the right.

It may also happen that a film is passed on from one mirror to another, so that as many as five or six images are produced. Objects tucked away in the inner part of a house, however long and winding the approach to their hiding place, can thus be brought into sight along devious routes by a series of mirrors. So the image is flashed from mirror to mirror. And on each occasion what is transmitted as the left becomes the right and is then again reversed and returns to its original relative position.

Again, mirrors with projecting sides whose curvature matches our own give back to us unreversed images. This may be because the film is thrown from one surface of the mirror to the other and reaches us only after a double rebound. Alternatively, it may be that on reaching the mirror the film is slewed round, because the curved surface gives it a twist towards us.

You would fancy that images walk along with us, keeping step and copying our gestures. This is because, as soon as you withdraw from a bit of the mirror, no films can be reflected from that part. Nature ordains that every particle shall rebound from the reflecting surface at an angle corresponding to its incidence.

Now for the fact that *the eyes avoid bright objects* and refuse to gaze at them. The sun, indeed, actually blinds them if you persist in directing them towards it. The reason is that its force is immense and the films it gives off travel with great momentum through a great depth of pure air and hit the eyes hard, so as to disrupt their atomic structure. Besides, a bright light that is painful often scorches the eyes, because it contains many particles of fire whose infiltration sets them smarting.

Sufferers from jaundice, again, *see everything they look at as yellow*. This is because many particles of yellowness from their own bodies are streaming out in the path of the approaching films. There are also many such particles blended in the structure of their own eyes, and by contamination with these everything is sullied with their sallowness.

When we are in the dark we see objects that are in the light for the following reason. The black murky air that lies nearer to us enters first into our open eyes and takes possession of them. It is then closely followed by bright and shining air, which cleanses them and dispels the shadows of the earlier air. For the bright air is many degrees more mobile and many degrees finer-grained and more potent. As soon as this has filled the passages of the eyes with light and opened

those that had previously been blockaded by dark air, they
are immediately followed by films thrown off from the
illuminated objects, and these stimulate our sense of sight.
On the other hand, when we look out of light into darkness,
we can see nothing: the murky air, of muddier consistency,
arrives last and chokes all the inlets of the eyes and
blockades their passages, so that they cannot be stirred
by the impact of films from any object.

*When we see the square towers of a city in the distance, they often
appear round.* This is because every angle seen at a distance
is blunted or even is not seen as an angle at all. Its impact is
nullified and does not penetrate as far as our eyes, because
films that travel through a great deal of air lose their sharp
outlines through frequent collisions with it. When every
angle has thus eluded our sense, the result is as though the
squared ashlars were rounded off on the lathe – not that they
resemble really round stones seen close up, but in a sketchy
sort of way they counterfeit them.

Again, *our shadow in the sunlight seems to us to move* and keep
step with us and imitate our gestures, incredible though it
is that unillumined air should walk about in conformity
with a man's movements and gestures. For what we commonly call a shadow can be nothing but air deprived of light.
Actually the earth is robbed of sunlight in a definite
succession of places wherever it is obstructed by us in our
progression, and the part we have left is correspondingly
replenished with it. That is why the successive shadows of
our body seem to be the same shadow following us along
steadily step by step. New particles of radiance are always
streaming down and their predecessors are consumed, as the
saying goes, like wool being spun into the fire. So the earth

is easily robbed of light and is correspondingly replenished and washes off the black stains of shadow.

Here, as always, *we do not admit that the eyes are in any way deluded*. It is their function to see where light is, and where shadow. But whether one light is the same as another, and whether the shadow that was here is moving over there, or whether on the other hand what really happens is what I have just described – that is something to be discerned by the reasoning power of the mind. The nature of phenomena cannot be understood by the eyes. You must not hold them responsible for this fault of the mind.

A ship in which we are sailing is on the move, though it seems to stand still. Another that rides at anchor gives the impression of sailing by. Hills and plains appear to be drifting astern when our ship soars past them with sails for wings.

The stars all seem motionless, embedded in the ethereal vault; yet they must all be in constant motion, since they rise and traverse the heavens with their luminous bodies till they return to the far-off scene of their setting. So too the sun and moon appear to remain at their posts, though the facts prove them travellers.

Mountains rising from the midst of the sea in the far distance, though there may be ample space between them for the free passage of a fleet, look as if linked together in a single island.

When children have come to a standstill after spinning round, they seem to see halls and pillars whirling round them – and so vividly that they can scarcely believe that the whole roof is not threatening to tumble on top of them.

When nature is just beginning to fling up the light of day, ruddy with flickering fires, and lift it high above the hill-tops, the glowing sun seems to perch upon the hills and kindle them by direct contact with its own fire. Yet these same hills are distant from us a bare two thousand bowshots – often indeed no more than five hundred javelin casts. But between hills and sun lie enormous tracts of ocean, overarched by vast ethereal vaults, and many thousand intervening lands, peopled by all the various races of men and beasts.

A puddle no deeper than a finger's breadth, formed in a hollow between the cobble-stones of the highway, offers to the eye a downward view, below the ground, of as wide a scope as the towering immensity of sky that yawns above. You would fancy you saw clouds far down below you and a sky and heavenly bodies deep-buried in a miraculous heaven beneath the earth.

When the mettlesome steed we are riding stands stock-still in midstream and we glance down at the swift-flowing torrent, our stationary mount seems to be breasting the flood and forcing its way rapidly upstream; and, wherever we cast our eyes, everything seems to be surging and forging ahead with the same movement as ourselves.

When we gaze from one end down the whole length of a colonnade, though its structure is perfectly symmetrical and it is propped throughout on pillars of equal height, yet it contracts by slow degrees in a narrowing cone that draws roof to floor and left to right till it unites them in the imperceptible apex of the cone.

To sailors at sea, the sun appears to rise out of the waves and to set in the waves and there hide its light. This is because they do in fact see only water and sky – another warning not to jump to the conclusion that the senses are shaky guides on all points.

To landsmen ignorant of the sea, ships in harbour seem to be riding crippled on the waves, with their poops broken. So much of the oars as projects above the waterline is straight, and so is the upper part of the rudder. But all the submerged parts appear refracted and wrenched round in an upward direction and almost as though bent right back so as to float on the surface.

At a time when scattered clouds are scudding before the wind across the night sky, the sparkling constellations look as though they were gliding along in the teeth of the clouds and passing overhead in a direction quite different from their actual course.

If we press our hand against one eye from below, a new sort of perception results. Whatever we look at, we see double: the lamplight, aflower with flame, becomes twin lights; the furniture throughout the house is doubled; men wear double faces and two bodies apiece.

When sleep has fettered all our limbs in the pleasant chains of slumber, and the whole body has sunk in utter tranquillity, we still seem to ourselves to be wide awake and moving our limbs. In the pitch blackness of night we fancy ourselves gazing on the sun and the broad light of day. In a confined space, we seem to traverse sky and sea, rivers and mountains, and wander afoot over prairies. With the solemn hush of night all around, we listen to sounds; we speak aloud without a word uttered.

We have many other paradoxical experiences of the same kind, all of which seem bent on shaking our faith in the senses. But all to no purpose. Most of this illusion is due to the mental assumptions which we ourselves superimpose, so that things not perceived by the senses pass for perceptions. There is nothing harder than to separate the facts as revealed from the questionable interpretations promptly imposed on them by the mind.

If anyone thinks that nothing can be known, he does not know whether even this can be known, since he admits that he knows nothing. Against such an adversary, therefore, who deliberately stands on his head, I will not trouble to argue my case. And yet, if I were to grant that he possessed this knowledge, I might ask several pertinent questions. Since he has had no experience of truth, how does he know the difference between knowledge and ignorance? What has originated the concept of truth and falsehood? Where is his proof that doubt is not the same as certainty?

You will find, in fact, that the concept of truth was originated by the senses and that the senses cannot be rebutted. The testimony that we must accept as more trustworthy is that which can spontaneously overcome falsehood with truth. What then are we to pronounce more trustworthy than the senses? Can reason derived from the deceitful senses be invoked to contradict them, when it is itself wholly derived from the senses? If they are not true, then reason in its entirety is equally false. Or can hearing give the lie to sight, or touch to hearing? Can touch in turn be discredited by taste or refuted by the nostrils or rebutted by the eyes? This, in my view, is out of the question. Each sense has its own distinctive faculty, its specific function. There must be separate discernment of softness and cold and heat and of the various colours of things and whatever goes with the colours; separate functioning of the palate's power of taste; separate generation of scents and sounds. This rules out the possibility of one sense confuting another. It will be equally out of the question for one sense to belie itself, since it will always be entitled to the same degree of credence. Whatever the senses may perceive at any time is all alike true. Suppose that reason cannot elucidate the cause why things that were square when close at hand are seen as round in the distance. Even so, it is better, in default of reason, to assign fictitious causes to the two shapes than to let things clearly apprehended slip from our grasp. This is to attack belief at its very roots – to tear up the entire foundation on which the maintenance of life is built. It is not only reason that would collapse completely. If you did not dare trust your senses so as to keep clear of precipices and other such things to be avoided and make for their opposites, there would be a speedy end to life itself.

So all this armament that you have marshalled against the senses is nothing but a futile array of words. If you set out to construct a building with a crooked ruler, a faulty square that is set a little out of the straight and a level ever so slightly askew, there can be only one outcome – a crazy, rickety, higgledy-piggledy huddle, sagging here and bulging there, with bits that look like falling at any moment and all in fact destined to fall, doomed by the initial miscalculations on which the structure is based. Just as rickety and just as defective must be the structure of your reasoning, if the senses on which it rests are themselves deceptive.

After this the problem that next confronts us – to determine *how each of the remaining senses perceives its own objects* – is not a particularly thorny one.

In the first place, all forms of *sound and vocal utterance* become audible when they have slipped into the ear and provoked sensation by the impact of their own bodies. The fact that voices and other sounds can impinge on the senses is itself a proof of their corporeal nature. Besides, the voice often scrapes the throat and a shout roughens the windpipe on its outward path. What happens is that, when atoms of voice in greater numbers than usual have begun to squeeze out through the narrow outlet, the doorway of the overcrowded mouth gets scraped. Undoubtedly, if voices and words have this power of causing pain, they must consist of corporeal particles. Again, you must have noticed how much it takes out of a man, and what wear and tear it causes to his thews and sinews, to keep on talking from the first glow of dawn till the evening shadows darken, especially if his words are uttered at the pitch of his voice. Since much talking actually takes something out of the body, it follows that voice is composed of bodily stuff. Finally, the harshness of a sound is due to the harshness of its component atoms, and its smoothness to their smoothness. There is a marked difference in the shape of the atoms that enter our ears when a low-toned trumpet booms its *basso profondo* and the hoarse-throated roar re-echoes from savage crags, and when the swans' plaintive dirge floats up in doleful melody from the winding glens of Helicon.

When we force out these utterances from the depths of our body and launch them through the direct outlet of the mouth, they are cut up into lengths by the flexible tongue, the craftsman of words, and moulded in turn by the configuration of the lips. At a point reached by each particular utterance after travelling no great distance from its source, it naturally happens that the individual words are also clearly audible and distinguishable syllable by syllable. For the utterance preserves its shape and configuration. But if the intervening space is unduly wide, the words must inevitably be jumbled and the utterance disjointed by its flight through a long stretch of gusty air. So it happens that, while you are aware of a sound, you cannot discern the sense of the words: the utterance comes to you so muddled and entangled.

It often happens that a single word, uttered from the mouth of a crier, penetrates the ears of a whole crowd.

Evidently, a single utterance must split up immediately into a multitude of utterances, since it is parcelled out amongst a number of separate ears, imprinting upon each the shape of a word and its distinctive sound. Such of these utterances as do not strike upon the ears float by and are scattered to the winds and lost without effect. Some of them, however, bump against solid objects and bounce back, so as to carry back a sound and sometimes mislead with the replica of a word. Once you have grasped this, you can explain to yourself and to others how it is that in desert places, when we are searching for comrades who have scattered and strayed among overshadowed glens and hail them at the pitch of our voices, the cliffs fling back the forms of our words in due sequence. I have observed places tossing back six or seven utterances when you have launched a single one: with their tendency to rebound, the words were reverberated and reiterated from hill to hill. According to local legend, these places are haunted by goat-footed Satyrs and by Nymphs. Tales are told of Fauns, whose noisy revels and merry pranks shatter the mute hush of night for miles around; of twanging lyre-strings and plaintive melodies poured out by flutes at the touch of the players' fingers; of music far-heard by the country-folk when Pan, tossing the pine-branches that wreathe his brutish head, runs his arched lips again and again along the wide-mouthed reeds, so that the pipe's wildwood rhapsody flows on unbroken. Many such fantasies and fairy tales are related by the rustics. Perhaps, in boasting of these marvels, they hope to dispel the notion that they live in backwoods abandoned even by the gods. Perhaps they have some other motive, since mankind everywhere has greedy ears for such romancing.

There remains the problem, not a very puzzling one, of

how sounds can penetrate and strike on the ear through media through which objects cannot be clearly perceived by the eye. The obvious reason why we often see a conversation going on through closed doors is that an utterance can make its way intact through circuitous fissures in objects impervious to visual films. For these are broken up, unless they are passing through straight fissures such as those in glass, which is penetrable by any sort of image. Again, sounds are disseminated in all directions because each one, after its initial splintering into a great many parts, gives birth to others, just as a spark of fire often propagates itself by starting fires of its own. So places out of the direct path are often filled with voices, which surge round every obstacle, one sound being provoked by another. But visual films all continue in straight lines along their initial paths, so that no one can see over a wall, as he can hear voices from inside it. Even a voice, however, is blunted in its passage through barriers and reaches our ears blurred, so that we seem to hear a mere noise rather than words.

As for the organs of *taste*, the tongue and the palate, they do not call for lengthier explanation or more expenditure of labour. In the first place, we perceive taste in the mouth when we squeeze it out by chewing food, just as if someone were to grasp a sponge full of water in his hand and begin to squeeze it dry. Next, all that we squeeze out is diffused through the pores of the palate and the winding channels of the spongy tongue. When the trickling particles of savour are smooth, they affect the palate pleasantly and pleasantly tickle all the moist regions of the tongue in their circuitous flow. Others, in proportion as their shape is rougher, tend more to prick and tear the organs of sense by their entry.

The pleasure derived from taste does not extend beyond

the palate. When the tasty morsel has all been gulped down the gullet and is being distributed through the limbs, it gives no more pleasure. It does not matter a rap what food you take to nourish your body so long as you can digest it and distribute it through your limbs and preserve the right balance of fluid in the stomach.

Let me now explain why one man's meat is not another's, and what is bitter and unpalatable to one may strike another as highly agreeable. The difference in reaction is indeed so great that what is food to one may be literally poison to others. There is, for instance, a snake that is so affected by contact with human spittle that it bites itself to death. To us hellebore is rank poison; but goats and quails grow fat on it. In order to understand how this happens, the first point to remember is one that I have already mentioned, the diversity of atoms that are commingled in objects. With the outward differences between the various types of animal that take food – the specific distinctions revealed by the external contour of their limbs – there go corresponding differences in the shapes of their component atoms. These in their turn entail differences in the chinks and channels – the pores, as we call them – in all parts of the body, including the mouth and the palate itself. In some species these are naturally smaller, in others larger; in some triangular, in others square; while many are round, others are of various polygonal shapes. In short, the shapes and motions of the atoms rigidly determine the shapes of the pores: the atomic structure defines the interatomic channels. When something sweet to one is bitter to another, it must be because its smoothest particles palpably penetrate the palate of the former, whereas the latter's gullet is evidently invaded by particles that are rough and jagged. On this basis the whole problem becomes easily soluble. Thus, when some person is afflicted with fever through superfluity of bile, or sickness is provoked in him by some other factor, his entire body is simultaneously upset and all the positions of the component atoms are changed. It follows that particles which used to be conformable to the channels of his sense are so no longer, whereas an easier ingress is afforded to those other particles whose entry can provoke a disagreeable sensation. For, as I have already demonstrated many times, the flavour of honey actually consists of a mixture of both kinds, pleasant and unpleasant.

Let me now tackle the question *how the nostrils are affected by the impact of smell.*

First, then, there must be a multitude of objects giving off a multifarious effluence of smells, which is to be conceived as emitted in a stream and widely diffused. But particular smells, owing to their distinctive shapes, are better adapted to particular species of animals. Bees are attracted for unlimited distances through the air by the smell of honey, vultures by carcasses. Where the cloven hoof of wild game has planted its spoor, the hunter is guided by his vanguard of hounds. The scent of man is detected far in advance by that lily-white guardian of Romulus' citadel, the goose. So each by its own particular gift of smell is attracted to its proper food or repelled from noxious poison; and thus the various species are preserved.

This specific adaptability is not confined to smells and tastes. The visible forms and colours of things are not all equally conformable to the sense organs of all species, but in some cases particular sights act rather as irritants. The sight of a cock, that herald of the dawn who banishes the night with clapping wings and lusty crowing, is intolerable to ravening lions. At the first glimpse they think only of

flight. The reason is, of course, that the cock's body contains certain atoms which, when they get into the lion's
eyes, prick the eyeballs and cause acute pain, so that even
their bold spirits cannot long endure it. But these atoms
have no power to hurt our eyes, either because they never
get in at all or because, once in, they have a clear way out,
so that they do not hurt the eyeball by meeting obstruction
at any point.

To return to the smells that assail our nostrils, it is clear
that some of them have a longer range than others. None of
them, however, travels as far as voices or other sounds, not
to speak of the films that strike the eyeballs and provoke
sight. For smell is a straggling and tardy traveller and fades
away before arriving, by the gradual dissipation of its flimsy
substance into the gusty air. One reason for this is that
smell originates in the depths of objects and is thus given off
haltingly: an indication that odours thus seep out and
escape from the inner core of objects is the fact that everything smells more strongly when broken or crushed or
dissolved by fire. A further reason is that smell is evidently
composed of larger atoms than sound, since it does not
pass through stone walls which are readily permeable by
voices and other sounds. That is why you will not find it so
easy to locate the source of a smell as of a sound. The
effluence grows cold by dawdling through the air and does
not rush with its tidings to the senses hotfoot from its
source. So it is that hounds are often at fault and have to
cast round for the scent.

Let me now explain briefly *what it is that stimulates the
imagination and where those images come from that enter the
mind.*

My first point is this. There are a great many flimsy films

from the surface of objects flying about in a great many ways in all directions. When these encounter one another in the air, they easily amalgamate, like gossamer or gold-leaf. In comparison with those films that take possession of the eye and provoke sight, these are certainly of a much flimsier texture, since they penetrate through the chinks of the body and set in motion the delicate substance of the mind within and there provoke sensation. So it is that we see the composite shapes of Centaurs and Mermaids and dogs with as many heads as Cerberus, and phantoms of the dead whose bones lie in the embrace of earth. The fact is that the films flying about everywhere are of all sorts: some are produced spontaneously in the air itself; others are derived from various objects and composed by the amalgamation of their shapes. The image of a Centaur, for instance, is certainly not formed from the life, since no living creature of this sort ever existed. But, as I have just explained, where surface films from a horse and a man accidentally come into contact, they may easily stick together on the spot, because of the delicacy and flimsiness of their texture. So also with other such chimerical creatures. Since, as I have shown above, these delicate films move with the utmost nimbleness and mobility, any one of them may easily set our mind in motion with a single touch; for the mind itself is delicate and marvellously mobile.

The truth of this explanation may be easily inferred from the following facts. First, in so far as a vision beheld by the mind closely resembles one beheld by the eyes, the two must have been created in a similar fashion. Now, I have shown that I see a lion, for example, through the impact of films on the eyes. It follows that something similar accounts for the motion of the mind, which also, no less than the eyes, beholds a lion or whatever it may be by means of films. The only difference is that the objects of its vision are flimsier.

Again, when our limbs are relaxed in slumber, our mind is as wakeful as ever. The same sort of films impinge upon it then as when we are awake, but now with such vividness that in sleep we may even be convinced that we are seeing someone who has passed from life into the clutches of death and earth. This results quite naturally from the stoppage and quiescence of all the bodily senses throughout the frame, so that they cannot refute a false impression by true ones. The memory also is put out of action by sleep and does not protest that the person whom the mind fancies it sees alive has long since fallen into the power of death and dissolution. It is not surprising that dream images should move about with measured gestures of their arms and other limbs. When this happens, it means that one film has passed and is succeeded by another formed in a different posture, so that it seems as though the earlier image had changed its attitude. We must picture this succession as taking place at high speed: the films fly so quickly and are drawn from so many sources, and at any perceptible instant of time there are so many atoms to keep up the supply.

This subject raises various questions that we must elucidate if we wish to give a clear account of it.

The first question is this: Why is it that, as soon as the mind takes a fancy to think about some particular object, it promptly does so? Are we to suppose that images are waiting on our will, so that we have only to wish and the appropriate film immediately impinges on our mind, whether it be the sea that we fancy or the earth or the sky? Assemblages of men, processions, banquets, battles – does nature create all these at a word and make them ready for us? And we must remember that, at the same time and in the same place, the minds of others are contemplating utterly different objects.

Again, when in our dreams we see images walking with measured step and moving their supple limbs, why do they swing their supple arms in time with alternate legs and perform repeated movements with their feet appropriate to their shifting glances? Are we to suppose the stray films are imbued with art and trained to spend their nights in dancing?

Another answer can be given to both questions that is surely nearer the truth. In one perceptible instant of time, that is, the time required to utter a single syllable, there are many unperceived units of time whose existence is recognized by reason. That explains why, at any given time, every sort of film is ready to hand in every place: they fly so quickly and are drawn from so many sources. And, because they are so flimsy, the mind cannot distinctly perceive any but those it makes an effort to perceive. All the rest pass without effect, leaving only those for which the mind has prepared itself. And the mind prepares itself in the expectation of seeing each appearance followed by its natural sequel. So this, in fact, is what it does see. You must have noticed how even our eyes, when they set out to look at inconspicuous objects, make an effort and prepare themselves; otherwise it is not possible for us to perceive distinctly. And, even when you are dealing with visible objects, you will find that, unless you direct your mind towards them, they have about them all the time an air of detachment and remoteness. What wonder, then, if the mind misses every impression except those to which it surrenders itself? The result is that we draw sweeping conclusions from trifling indications and lead ourselves into pitfalls of delusion.

Sometimes it happens that an image is not forthcoming to match our expectation: what was a woman seems to be suddenly transformed into a man before our eyes, or we are confronted by some swift change of feature or age. Any surprise we might feel at this is checked by drowsy for-getfulness.

In this context, there is one illusion that you must do your level best to escape – an error to guard against with all your foresight. You must not imagine that the bright orbs of our eyes were created purposely, so that we might be able to look before us; that our need to stride ahead determined our equipment with the pliant props of thigh and ankle, set in the firm foundation of our feet; that our arms were fitted to stout shoulders, and helpful hands attached at either side, in order that we might do what is needful to sustain life. To interpret these or any other phenomena on these lines is perversely to turn the truth upside down. In fact, *nothing in our bodies was born in order that we might be able to use it, but the thing born creates the use.* There was no seeing before eyes were born, no talking before the tongue was created. The origin of the tongue was far anterior to speech. The ears were created long before a sound was heard. All the limbs, I am well assured, existed before their use. They cannot, therefore, have grown for the sake of being used.

Battles were fought hand to hand, limbs were mangled and bodies fouled with blood long before flashing spears were hurled. Wounds were parried at the bidding of nature before the left arm interposed a shield through the agency of art. Yes, and laying the weary frame to rest is an earlier institution than spreading comfortable beds, and thirst was quenched before ever cups were thought of. We can believe, therefore, that these instruments, whose invention sprang from need and life, have been designed to serve a purpose. Quite different are those organs that were first born themselves and afterwards provided a mental picture of their own functioning. And prominent in this latter class we find our sense-organs and bodily members. Here, then, is proof upon proof that you must banish the belief that they could have been created for the purpose of performing particular functions.

Another fact that need occasion no surprise is that *the body of every living creature by its own nature seeks after food.* I have already shown that countless particles in countless ways are passing off in a stream from all objects. But the greatest number of all must be emitted by animals. Since animals are always on the move, they lose a great many atoms, some squeezed out from the inner depths by the process of perspiration, some breathed out through the mouth when they gasp and pant. By these processes the body's density is diminished and its substance sapped. This results in pain. Hence food is taken so that, when duly distributed through limbs and veins, it may underpin the frame and rebuild its strength and sate its open-mouthed lust for eating. Moisture is similarly diffused into all the members that demand moisture; and the many accumulated particles of heat that inflame our stomach are dispelled by the advent of the fluid and quenched like a fire, so that the frame is no longer parched by burning drought. So it is that the thirst that sets you gasping is swilled out of the body and the craving of hunger glutted.

Let me now explain *how it comes about that we can stride forward at will and are empowered to move our limbs* in various ways, and what it is that has learnt to lift along this heavy load of our body. I count on you to mark my words. I will begin by repeating my previous statement that images of walking come to our mind and impinge upon it. Hence comes the will. For no one ever initiates any action without the mind first foreseeing what it wills. What it foresees is the substance of the image. So the mind, when the motions it experiences are such that it wishes to step forward, immediately jogs the vital spirit diffused through every limb and organ of the body. This is easily done, since mind and spirit are interconnected. The spirit in turn then jogs the body. And so bit by bit the whole bulk is pushed forward and set in motion.

A further effect is that the body grows less dense. The opened pores admit air, as is natural, since this is always highly mobile. The air rushes in in a stream and is thus diffused into every part of the body, however small. From the combination of these two factors it results that the body is pushed along, just as a ship is propelled by the combined action of wind and sails.

There is no need to be surprised that bodies so minute can twist round a body of such bulk and divert the course of our whole weight. The wind is tenuous enough, and its particles are diminutive; but it shoves along the mighty mass of a mighty ship, and, however much way it has gathered, a single hand steers it – a single tiller twists it this way or that. And many a heavy load is shifted and hoisted with an easy swing by a derrick, with the aid of pulleys and winches.

And now for *the problem of sleep:* by what contrivance does it flood our limbs with peace and unravel from our breasts the mind's disquietude? My answer will be persuasive rather than exhaustive: better the fleeting melody of the swan than the long-drawn clangour of cranes high up among the northward-racing clouds. It rests with you to lend an unresisting ear and an inquiring mind. Otherwise you may refuse to accept my explanation as possible and walk away with a mind that flings back the truth, though the blame lies with your own blindness.

In the first place, sleep occurs when the vital spirit throughout the body is discomposed: when part of it has been forced out and lost, part compressed and driven into the inner depths. At such times the limbs are unknit and grow limp. For undoubtedly the sensibility that is in us is caused by the spirit. When sensation is deadened by sleep, we must suppose that this is due to the derangement of the spirit or its expulsion. But it is not all expelled, or else the body would be steeped in the everlasting chill of death. If there were really no lurking particle of spirit left in the limbs, as smothered fire lurks in a heap of ashes, from what source could sentience be suddenly rekindled in the limbs, as flame leaps up from hidden fire? I will explain how this change is brought about and how the spirit can be deranged and the body grow limp. You must see to it that I do not waste my words on the wind.

First, then, a body on its outer surface borders on the gusty air and is touched by it. It must therefore be pelted by it with a continual rain of blows. That is why almost all bodies are covered with hide or shell, rind or bark. In bodies that breathe, the interior also is battered by air as it is inhaled and exhaled. Since our body is thus bombarded outside and in and the blows penetrate through little pores to its primary parts and primal elements, our limbs are subject in a sense to a gradual crumbling. The atoms of body and mind are dislodged from their stations. The result is that part of the spirit is forced out; part becomes tucked away in the interior; part is loosely scattered throughout

the limbs, so that it cannot unite or engage in interacting
motions, because nature interposes obstacles to combination
and movement. This deep-seated change in motion means
the withdrawal of sentience. At the same time, since there
is some lack of matter to support the frame, the body grows
weak; all the limbs slacken; arms and eyelids droop; often,
when a man is seeking rest, his knees lose their strength and
give way under him.

Food, again, induces sleepiness, because its action, when
it is being distributed through all the veins, is the same as
that of air. The heaviest kind of sleep is that which ensues
on satiety or exhaustion, since it is then that the atoms are
thrown into the greatest confusion under stress of their
heavy labour. The same cause makes the partial congestion
of spirit more deep-seated and the evacuation more extensive, and aggravates the internal separation and dislocation.

Whatever employment has the strongest hold on our
interest or has last filled our waking hours, so as to engage
the mind's attention, that is what seems most often to keep
us occupied in sleep. Lawyers argue cases and frame contracts. Generals lead their troops into action. Sailors
continue their pitched battle with the winds. And as for me,
I go on with my task, for ever exploring the nature of the
universe and setting down my discoveries in my native
tongue. The same principle generally applies when other
crafts and occupations are observed to beguile men's minds
in sleep.

Similarly when men have devoted themselves whole-
heartedly for days on end to entertainments, we usually find
that the objects that have ceased to engage the senses have
left wide open channels in the mind for the entry of their
own images. So for many days the same sights hover before
their eyes: even when awake, they seem to see figures

dancing and swaying supple limbs; to fill their ears with the
liquid melody and speaking notes of the lyre, and to watch
the same crowded theatre, its stage ablaze with many-tinted
splendour.

Such is the striking effect of interest and pleasure and
customary employment, and not on men only but on all
animals. You will see mettlesome steeds, when their limbs
are at rest, still continuing in sleep to sweat and pant as if
straining all their strength to win the palm, or as if the lifted
barriers of the starting-post had just released them. And the
huntsman's hounds, while wrapped in gentle slumber, often
toss their legs with a quick jerk and utter sudden whines
and draw rapid breaths of air into their nostrils as if they
were hot on a newly-found scent. Even when awake, they
often chase after shadowy images of stags, as though they saw
them in full flight, till they shake off the illusion and return
to themselves. A litter of good-tempered house-bred pup-
pies are all agog to wriggle their bodies and heave them from
the ground, just as if they were seeing the forms and faces
of strangers. The fiercer the breed, the more savage must
be their behaviour in sleep. The various races of birds take
to flight and startle the groves of the gods at dead of night
with a sudden whirr of wings. Doubtless their restful
slumber is disturbed by visions of hawks swooping to the
fray in fierce pursuit.

Very similar as a rule is the behaviour in sleep of human
minds, whose massive motions are proportioned to massive
effect. Kings take cities by storm, are themselves taken
captive, join in battle and cry aloud as though they felt the
assassin's dagger – and all without stirring from the spot.
There are many who fight for their lives, giving vent to
their agony in groans or filling the night with piercing
screams as though they were writhing in the jaws of a

panther or a ravening lion. Many talk in their sleep about
matters of great moment and have often betrayed their own
guilt. Many meet their death. Many, who feel themselves
hurled bodily down to earth from towering crags, are startled
out of sleep; like men who have lost their wits, they are slow
in returning to themselves, so shaken are they by the tumult
of their body. The thirsty man finds himself seated beside a
river or a delectable spring and is near to gulping down the
whole stream. Little boys often fancy when fast asleep that
they are standing at a lavatory or a chamber pot and lifting
up their clothes. Then they discharge all the filtered fluid
of their body, and even the costly splendour of oriental
coverlets does not escape a soaking. Those on the verge of
manhood, in whose limbs the seed created by maturing age
is beginning to gather, are invaded from without by images
emanating from various bodies with tidings of an alluring
face and a delightful complexion. This stimulates the organs
swollen with an accumulation of seed. Often, as though
their function were actually fulfilled, they discharge a flood
of fluid and drench their covering.

In this last case, as I have explained, the thing in us that
responds to the stimulus is the seed that comes with ripening years and strengthening limbs. For different things
respond to different stimuli or provocations. *The one stimulus
that evokes human seed from the human body is a human form.* As
soon as this seed is dislodged from its resting-place, it
travels through every member of the body, concentrating at
certain reservoirs in the loins, and promptly acts upon the
generative organs. These organs are stimulated and swollen
by the seed. Hence follows the will to eject it in the direction in which tyrannical lust is tugging. The body makes for
the source from which the mind is pierced by love. For the

wounded normally fall in the direction of their wound: the
blood spurts out towards the source of the blow; and the
enemy who delivered it, if he is fighting at close quarters,
is bespattered by the crimson stream. So, when a man is
pierced by the shafts of Venus, whether they are launched
by a lad with womanish limbs or a woman radiating love
from her whole body, he strives towards the source of the
wound and craves to be united with it and to transmit
something of his own substance from body to body. His
speechless yearning is a presentiment of bliss.

This, then, is what we term Venus. This is the origin of
the thing called love – that drop of Venus' honey that first
drips into our heart, to be followed by numbing heart-ache.
Though the object of your love may be absent, images of it
still haunt you and the beloved name chimes sweetly in your
ears. If you find yourself thus passionately enamoured of an
individual, you should keep well away from such images.
Thrust from you anything that might feed your passion, and
turn your mind elsewhere. Vent the seed of love upon other
objects. By clinging to it you assure yourself the certainty of
heart-sickness and pain. With nourishment the festering sore
quickens and strengthens. Day by day the frenzy heightens
and the grief deepens. Your only remedy is to lance the
first wound with new incisions; to salve it, while it is still
fresh, with promiscuous attachments; to guide the motions
of your mind into some other channel.

Do not think that by avoiding grand passions you are
missing the delights of Venus. Rather, you are reaping such
profits as carry with them no penalty. Rest assured that this
pleasure is enjoyed in a purer form by the healthy than by
the love-sick. Lovers' passion is storm-tossed, even in the
moment of fruition, by waves of delusion and incertitude.
They cannot make up their mind what to enjoy first with

eye or hand. They clasp the object of their longing so tightly that the embrace is painful. They kiss so fiercely that teeth are driven into lips. All this because their pleasure is not pure, but they are goaded by an underlying impulse to hurt the thing, whatever it may be, that gives rise to these budding shoots of madness.

In the actual presence of love Venus lightens the penalties she imposes, and her sting is assuaged by an admixture of alluring pleasure. For in love there is the hope that the flame of passion may be quenched by the same body that kindled it. But this runs clean counter to the course of nature. This is the one thing of which the more we have, the more our breast burns with the evil lust of having. Food and fluid are taken into our body; since they can fill their allotted places, the desire for meat and drink is thus easily appeased. But a pretty face or a pleasing complexion gives the body nothing to enjoy but insubstantial images, which all too often fond hope scatters to the winds.

When a thirsty man tries to drink in his dreams but is given no drop to quench the fire in his limbs, he clutches at images of water with fruitless effort and while he laps up a rushing stream he remains thirsty in the midst. Just so in the midst of love Venus teases lovers with images. They cannot glut their eyes by gazing on the beloved form, however closely. Their hands glean nothing from those dainty limbs in their aimless roving over all the body. Then comes the moment when with limbs entwined they pluck the flower of youth. Their bodies thrill with the presentiment of joy, and it is seed-time in the fields of Venus. Body clings greedily to body; moist lips are pressed on lips, and deep breaths are drawn through clenched teeth. But all to no purpose. One can glean nothing from the other, nor enter in and be wholly absorbed, body in body; for sometimes it seems that that is what they are craving and striving to do, so hungrily do they cling together in Venus' fetters, while their limbs are unnerved and liquefied by the intensity of rapture. At length, when the spate of lust is spent, there comes a slight intermission in the raging fever. But not for long. Soon the same frenzy returns. The fit is upon them once more. They ask themselves what it is they are craving for, but find no device that will master their malady. In aimless bewilderment they waste away, stricken by an unseen wound.

Add to this that they spend their strength and fail under the strain. Their days are passed at the mercy of another's whim. Their wealth slips from them, transmuted to Babylonian brocades. Their duties are neglected. Their reputation totters and goes into a decline. It is all very well for dainty feet to sparkle with gay slippers of Sicyon; for settings of gold to enclasp huge emeralds aglow with green fire, and sea-tinted garments to suffer the constant wear and stain of Venus. A hard-won patrimony is metamorphosed into bonnets and tiaras or, it may be, into Grecian robes, masterpieces from the looms of Elis or of Ceos. No matter how lavish the décor and the cuisine – drinking parties (with no lack of drinks), entertainments, perfumes, garlands, festoons and all – they are still to no purpose. From the very heart of the fountain of delight there rises a jet of bitterness that poisons the fragrance of the flowers. Perhaps the unforgetting mind frets itself remorsefully with the thought of life's best years squandered in sloth and debauchery. Perhaps the beloved has let fly some two-edged word, which lodges in the impassioned heart and glows there like a living flame. Perhaps he thinks she is rolling her eyes too freely and turning them upon another, or he catches in her face a hint of mockery.

And these are the evils inherent in love that prospers and fulfils its hopes. In starved and thwarted love the evils you can see plainly without even opening your eyes are past all counting. How much better to be on your guard beforehand, as I have advised, and take care that you are not enmeshed!

To avoid enticement into the snares of love is not so difficult as, once entrapped, to escape out of the toils and snap the tenacious knots of Venus. And yet, be you never so tightly entangled and embrangled, you can still free yourself from the curse unless you stand in the way of your own freedom. First, you should concentrate on all the faults of mind or body of her whom you covet and sigh for. For men often behave as though blinded by love and credit the beloved with charms to which she has no valid title. How often do we see blemished and unsightly women basking in a lover's adoration! One man scoffs at another and urges him to propitiate Venus because he is the victim of such a degrading passion; yet as like as not the poor devil is in the same unhappy plight himself, all unaware. A sallow wench is acclaimed as a nut-brown maid. A sluttish slattern is admired for her 'sweet disorder'. Her eyes are never green, but grey as Athene's. If she is stringy and woody, she is lithe as a gazelle. A stunted runt is a sprite, a sheer delight from top to toe. A clumsy giantess is 'a daughter of the gods divinely tall'. She has an impediment in her speech – a charming lisp, of course. She's as mute as a stockfish – what modesty! A waspish, fiery-tempered scold – she 'burns with a gem-like flame'. She becomes 'svelte' and 'willowy' when she is almost too skinny to live; 'delicate' when she is half-dead with coughing. Her breasts are swollen and protuberant: she is 'Ceres suckling Bacchus'. Her nose is snub – 'a Faun', then, or 'a child of the Satyrs'. Her lips bulge: she is 'all kiss'. It would be a wearisome task to run through the whole catalogue. But suppose her face in fact is all that could be desired and the charm of Venus radiates from her whole body. Even so, there are still others. Even so, we lived without her before. Even so, in her physical nature she is no different, as we well know, from the plainest of her sex. She is driven to use foul-smelling fumigants. Her maids keep well away from her and snigger behind her back. The tearful lover, shut out from the presence, heaps the threshold with flowers and garlands, anoints the disdainful door-posts with perfume, and plants rueful kisses on the door. Often enough, were he admitted, one whiff would promptly make him cast round for some decent pretext to take his leave. His fond complaint, long-pondered and far-fetched, would fall dismally flat. He would curse himself for a fool to have endowed her with qualities above mortal imperfection.

To the daughters of Venus themselves all this is no secret. Hence they are at pains to hide all the back-stage activities of life from those whom they wish to keep fast bound in the bonds of love. But their pains are wasted, since your mind has power to drag all these mysteries into the daylight and get at the truth behind the sniggers. Then, if the lady is good-hearted and void of malice, it is up to you in your turn to accept unpleasant facts and make allowance for human imperfection.

Do not imagine that a woman is always sighing with feigned love when she clings to a man in a close embrace, body to body, and prolongs his kisses by the tension of moist lips. Often she is acting from the heart and in longing for a shared delight tempts him to run love's race to the end. So, too, with birds and beasts, both tame and wild. Cows and mares would never submit to the males, were it not that their female nature in its superabundance is all aglow and their resistance to the generative seed is quelled by delight. Have you never noticed, again, how couples linked by mutual rapture are often tormented in their common bondage? How often dogs at a street corner, wishing to separate, tug lustily with all their might in opposite directions and yet remain united by the constraining fetters of Venus? This they would never do unless they experienced mutual joys which mock at their efforts and hold them enchained. Here then is proof upon proof for my contention that the pleasure of sex is shared.

In the intermingling of seed it may happen that the woman by a sudden effort overmasters the power of the man and takes control of it. Then children are conceived of the maternal seed and take after their mother. Correspondingly children may be conceived of the paternal seed and take after their father. The children in whom you see a two-sided likeness, combining features of both parents, are products alike of their father's body and their mother's blood. At their making the seeds that course through the limbs under the impulse of Venus were dashed together by the collusion of mutual passion in which neither party was master or mastered.

It may also happen at times that children take after their grandparents, or recall the features of great-grandparents. This is because the parents' bodies often preserve a quantity of latent seeds, grouped in many combinations, which derive from an ancestral stock handed down from generation to generation. From these Venus evokes a random assortment of characters, reproducing ancestral traits of expression, voice or hair; for these characters are determined by specific seeds no less than our faces and bodily members.

It may seem strange that female offspring is engendered from the father's seed, and the mother's body gives birth to males. The fact is that the embryo is always composed of atoms from both sources, only it derives more than half from the parent which it more closely resembles. This is noticeable in either case, whether the child's origin is predominantly male or female.

Do not imagine that fruitful seed is denied to any man by the will of the gods, so that he may never be hailed as father by winsome children but must live through a sexual life that yields no fruit. There are many who are moved by this belief to enrich the sacrificial altars with rivers of blood and the smoke of burnt offerings in the pathetic hope that their wives may be made big with unstinted seed. It is all in vain that they importune gods or fates. For the barrenness of the males is due in some cases to the over-coarse grain of the seed, in others to its excessive fineness and fluidity. The fine seed, because it cannot stick fast in its place, slips quickly away and returns abortive. The coarser type, because it is emitted in too cohesive a form, either does not travel with enough momentum, or fails to penetrate where it is required or else, having got there, fails to mix properly with the female seed. For the affairs of Venus clearly involve wide variations in harmony. Men differ in their power to impregnate different women, and women similarly in the power to receive from different men and grow big by them. Many women have proved barren in earlier unions yet have eventually found husbands by whom they could conceive little ones and be enriched with the blessings of childbirth. And men in whose homes fruitful women have previously failed to bear have at length found a complementary nature so that they too could fortify their declining years with sons.

The vital thing is to ensure the right mixture of seeds for

procreation, coarse harmonizing with fine and fine with coarse. Another important factor is diet: some foods thicken the seeds in the body, others in turn thin and diminish them. A third factor of great importance is the mode in which the pleasures of intercourse are enjoyed. It is thought that women conceive more readily in the manner of four-footed beasts in a prone posture with loins uplifted so as to give access to the seed. Certainly, wives have no need of lascivious movements. A woman makes conception more difficult by offering a mock resistance and accepting Venus with a wriggling body. She diverts the furrow from the straight course of the ploughshare and makes the seed fall wide of the plot. These tricks are employed by prostitutes for their own ends, so that they may not conceive too frequently and be laid up by pregnancy and at the same time may make intercourse more attractive to men. But obviously our wives can have no use for them.

Lastly, it is by no divine intervention, no prick of Cupid's darts, that a woman deficient in beauty sometimes becomes the object of love. Often the woman herself, by humouring a man's fancies and keeping herself fresh and smart, makes it easy for him to share his life with her. Over and above this, love is built up bit by bit by mere usage. Nothing can resist the continually repeated impact of a blow, however light, as you see drops of water falling on one spot at long last wear through a stone.

Book V

COSMOLOGY AND SOCIOLOGY

*

WHO has such power within his breast that he could build up a song worthy of this high theme and these discoveries? Who has such mastery of words that he could praise as he deserves the man who produced such treasures from his breast and bequeathed them to us? No one, I believe, whose body is of mortal growth. If I am to suit my language to the majesty of his revelations, he was a god – a god indeed, my noble Memmius – who first discovered that rule of life that now is called *philosophy*, who by his art rescued life from such a stormy sea, so black a night, and steered it into such a calm and sun-lit haven. Only compare with his achievement those ancient discoveries of other mortals that rank as the work of gods. Ceres, it is said, taught men to use cereals, and Bacchus the juice of the grape; yet without these things we could go on living, as we are told that some tribes live even now. But life could not be well lived till our breasts were swept clean. Therefore that man has a better claim to be called a god whose gospel, broadcast through the length and breadth of empires, is even now bringing soothing solace to the minds of men.

As for Hercules, if you think his deeds will challenge comparison, you will stray farther still from the path of truth. The gaping jaws of that Nemean lion, or the bristly Arcadian boar – what harm could they do us now? Or the Cretan bull

and the Hydra with its palisade of venomous snakes, the pest
of Lerna? What would it matter to us if Geryon, with the
triple strength of his three bodies, still lorded it in farthest
Spain, or the foul birds haunted the Stymphalian mere, or
Thracian Diomede's horses breathed fire from their nostrils
on the Balkan slopes of Ismara? Or if the scaly, fierce-eyed
serpent guarded still the lustrous golden apples of the
Hesperides, hugging the tree-trunk with huge coils, there
by the forbidding Atlantic shore where none of us ever goes
nor even the natives venture? And the other monsters of
this sort that met their death – if they had not been mastered,
what harm would they do alive? None at all, that I can see.
Even now the world swarms with wild beasts, enough and
to spare – a thrill of terror lurking in thickets on the mountain side or in the depths of forests. Only, we have little
occasion to go near their haunts. But, if our breasts are not
swept clean, then indeed what distracting and disruptive
forces we must let in! And, when a man harbours these,
what sharp stabs of desire with their answering fears tear
him to pieces! Pride, meanness, lust, self-indulgence, bore-
dom – what casualties they inflict! The man who has
defeated all these enemies and banished them from his
mind, by words not by weapons, is surely entitled to a place
among the gods. Remember, too, what inspired words he
himself has uttered about the immortal gods, and how by
his teaching he has laid bare the causes of things.

Treading in his footsteps, I have been running arguments
to earth and explaining in my verses the necessity that
compels everything to abide by the compact under which it
was created. For nothing has power to break the binding
laws of eternity. As an instance of this, I have shown that
the mind in particular is a natural growth: it is composed of

a body that had first to be born, and it cannot remain intact for all time; but we are misled by images in sleep, when we fancy we see someone whose life has left him.

The next stage in the argument is this. I must first demonstrate that the world also was born and is composed of a mortal body. Then I must deal with the concourse of matter that laid the foundation of land, sea and sky, stars and sun and the globe of the moon. I must show what living things have existed on earth, and which have never been born; how the human race began to employ various utterances among themselves for denoting various things; and how there crept into their minds that fear of the gods which, all the world over, sanctifies temples and lakes, groves and altars and images of the gods. After that, I will explain by what forces nature steers the courses of the sun and the journeyings of the moon, so that we shall not suppose that they run their yearly races between heaven and earth of their own free will with the amiable intention of promoting the growth of crops and animals, or that they are rolled round in furtherance of some divine plan. For it may happen that men who have learnt the truth about the carefree existence of the gods fall to wondering by what power the universe is kept going, especially those movements that are seen overhead in the borderland of ether. Then the poor creatures are plunged back into their old superstitions and saddle themselves with cruel masters whom they believe to be all-powerful. All this because they do not know what can be and what cannot: how a limit is fixed to the power of everything and an immovable frontier post.

And now, Memmius, I will not hold you off any longer with promises. First of all, then, cast your eyes on sea, lands and sky. These three bodies so different in nature, three distinct forms, three fabrics such as you behold – all these a single day will blot out. The whole substance and structure of the world, upheld through many years, will crash. I am well aware how novel and strange in its impact on the mind is this impending demolition of heaven and earth, and how hard it is for my words to carry conviction. This is always so when you bring to men's ears something outside their experience – something you cannot set before their eyes or lay hold of by hand, which is the shortest highway for belief to enter the human breast and the compartments of the mind. But, for all that, I will proclaim it. It may be that force will be given to my arguments by the event itself; that your own eyes will see those violent earthquakes in a brief space dash the whole world to fragments. From such a fate may guiding fortune steer us clear! May reason rather than the event itself convince you that the whole world can collapse with one ear-splitting crack!

Before I attempt to utter oracles on this theme, with more sanctity and far surer reason than those the Delphic prophetess pronounces, drugged by the laurel fumes from Apollo's tripod, I will first set your mind at rest with words of wisdom. Do not imagine, under the spell of superstition, that lands and sun and sky, sea, stars and moon, must endure for ever because they are endowed with a divine body. Do not for that reason think it right that punishment appropriate to a monstrous crime should be imposed, as on the rebellious Titans, on all those who by their reasoning breach the ramparts of the world and seek to darken heaven's brightest luminary, the sun, belittling with mortal speech immortal beings. In fact these objects are so far from divinity, so unworthy of a place among the gods, that they may rather serve to impress upon us the type of the lifeless and the insensible. Obviously, it is only with certain bodies that mind and intelligence can co-exist. A tree cannot exist in the ether, or clouds in the salt sea, as fishes cannot live in the fields or blood flow in wood or sap in stones. There is a determined and allotted place for the growth and presence of everything. So mind cannot arise alone without body or apart from sinews and blood. If it could do this, then surely it could much more readily function in head or shoulders or the tips of the heels or be born in any other part, so long as it was held in the same container, that is to say, in the same man. Since, however, even in the human body we see a determined and allotted place set aside for the growth and presence of spirit and mind, we have even stronger grounds for denying that they can survive apart from all body or animal form in the crumbling clods of earth or the fire of the sun or in water or the high borderland of ether. These objects, therefore, are not endowed with divine consciousness, since they cannot even possess living spirits.

Furthermore, you must not suppose that the holy dwelling-places of the gods are anywhere within the limits of the world. For the flimsy nature of the gods, far removed from our senses, is scarcely visible even to the perception of the mind. Since it eludes the touch and pressure of our hands, it can have no contact with anything that is tangible to us. For what cannot be touched cannot touch. Therefore their dwelling-places also must be unlike ours, of the same flimsy texture as their bodies, as I will prove to you at length later on.

Next, the theory that they deliberately created the world in all its natural splendour for the sake of man, so that we

ought to praise this eminently praiseworthy piece of divine
workmanship and believe it eternal and immortal and think
it a sin to unsettle by violence the everlasting abode established for mankind by the ancient purpose of the gods and
to worry it with words and turn it topsy-turvy – this theory,
Memmius, with all its attendant fictions is sheer nonsense.
For what benefit could immortal and blessed beings reap
from our gratitude, that they should undertake any task on
our behalf? Or what could tempt those who had been at
peace so long to change their old life for a new? The revolutionary is one who is dissatisfied with the old order. But one
who has known no trouble in the past, but spent his days
joyfully – what could prick such a being with the itch for
novelty? Or again, what harm would it have done us to
have remained uncreated? Are we to suppose that our life
was sunk in gloom and grief till the light of creation blazed
forth? True that, once a man is born, he must will to remain
alive so long as beguiling pleasure holds him. But one who
has never tasted the love of life, or been enrolled among the
living, what odds is it to him if he is never created?

Here is a further point. On what pattern did the gods
model their creation? From what source did an image of
human beings first strike upon them, so that they might
know and see with their minds what they wished to make?
How was the power of the atoms made known to them,
and the potential effect of their various combinations,
unless nature itself provided a model of the creation? So
many atoms, clashing together in so many ways as they are
swept along through infinite time by their own weight,
have come together in every possible way and realized
everything that could be formed by their combinations.
No wonder, then, if they have actually fallen into those

groupings and movements by which the present world through all its changes is kept in being.

Even if I knew nothing of the atoms, I would venture to assert on the evidence of the celestial phenomena themselves, supported by many other arguments, that the universe was certainly not created for us by divine power: it is so full of imperfections. In the first place, of all that is covered by the wide sweep of the sky, part has been greedily seized by mountains and the woodland haunts of wild beasts. Part is usurped by crags and desolate bogs and the sea that holds far asunder the shores of the lands. Almost two-thirds are withheld from mankind by torrid heat and perennial deposits of frost. The little that is left of cultivable soil, if the force of nature had its way, would be choked with briars, did not the force of man oppose it. It is man's way, for the sake of life, to groan over the stout mattock and cleave the earth with down-pressed plough. Unless we turn the fruitful clods with the coulter and break up the soil to stimulate the growth of the crops, they cannot emerge of their own accord into the open air. Even so, when by dint of hard work all the fields at last burst forth into leaf and flower, then either the fiery sun withers them with intemperate heat, or sudden showers and icy frosts destroy them and gales of wind batter them with hurricane force. Again, why does nature feed and breed the fearsome brood of wild beasts, a menace to the human race by land and sea? Why do the changing seasons bring pestilence in their train? Why does untimely death roam abroad? The human infant, like a shipwrecked sailor cast ashore by the cruel waves, lies naked on the ground, speechless, lacking all aids to life, when nature has first tossed him with pangs of travail from his mother's womb upon the shores of the sunlit world. He fills the air with his piteous wailing, and quite rightly, considering what evils life holds in store for him. But beasts of every kind, both tame and wild, have no need of rattles or a nurse to lull them with inarticulate babble. They do not want to change their clothes at every change in the weather. They need no armaments or fortifications to guard their possessions, since all the needs of all are lavishly supplied by mother earth herself and nature, the great artificer.

In the first place, *since the elements* of which we see the world composed – solid earth and moisture, the light breaths of air and torrid fire – *all consist of bodies that are neither birthless nor deathless, we must believe the same of the world as a whole.* It is a matter of observation that objects whose component parts consist of configurations of matter subject to birth and death are certainly not exempt themselves. So, when we see the main component members of the world disintegrated and reborn, it is a fair inference that sky and earth too had their birthday and will have their day of doom.

You need not tax me with begging the question when I assume that earth and fire are mortal and entertain no doubt about the death of wind and water or the rebirth and growth of all these elements.

Take the earth first. Part of it, parched by incessant sun and trampled by the tread of many feet, exhales a vapour and flying clouds of dust which strong winds scatter and commingle with the air. Part of the soil is reconverted to flood-water by the rains, and gnawing rivers nibble at their banks. And whatever earth contributes to feed the growth of others is restored to it. It is an observed fact that the universal mother is also the common grave. Earth, therefore, is whittled away and renewed with fresh increment.

As for water, it needs no words to show that sea and

river and springs are perennially replenished and the flow
of fluid is unending. The evidence confronts us everywhere
in the mighty downrush of water. But the vanguard of the
flood is perpetually skimmed away, and on balance the
surface-level does not rise. The sea is reduced in volume
partly by the strong winds that scour its surface, partly by
the fiery sun's dissolvent rays, partly because it seeps away
in all directions under the ground. The brine is filtered out,
and the main bulk of the water flows back and reassembles
in full at the fountainhead. Hence it flows overground, a
steady column of sweet fluid marching down the highway
already hewn with liquid foot for the guidance of its
waves.

Now a word about air, whose whole mass undergoes
innumerable transformations hour by hour. All the effluences that objects are for ever shedding are swept into the
vast ocean of air. Unless this in turn gave back matter to
objects and rebuilt their ever-flowing shapes, they would all
by now have been dissolved and turned to air. Accordingly it must be continuously generated from other things
and retransformed into them, since it is an established fact
that everything is in perpetual flux.

The fiery sun, too, the lavish fount of liquid light,
drenches the sky unwearyingly with fresh effulgence, never
tardy to replace old light with new. For each successive
flash of radiance, whatever may come of it, means a loss to
the fountainhead, as you may learn from the following
indication. No sooner do clouds begin to climb the sky and
cut off the rays of sunlight than all the lower part of the rays
immediately vanishes: wherever the clouds pass, the earth
is darkened. So you may gather that objects are always in
need of new illumination; that every burst of radiance is
short-lived; and that objects could never be seen in sunlight

if a perpetual supply were not maintained by the fount of light itself.

So it is with those earthly lights that illumine the night – swinging lamps and flaring torches, their bright flames thick with sooty smoke. Fed by their burning, they race to supply new light, pressing onward, onward, with ever-flickering flames, leaving no gap in the unbroken stream of brilliance: so hastily is its extinction hidden by the swift new birth of flame from every fire. That is how you should picture sun and moon and stars – as showering their splendour in successive outbursts and for ever losing flash after flash of flame, not as enduring essences untouched by time.

Look about you and you will see the very stones mastered by age; tall towers in ruin and their masonry crumbling; temples and images of the gods defaced, their destined span not lengthened by any sanctity that avails against the laws of nature. The monuments of the great seem to ask us why we look there for immortality. The uprooted boulders rolling down a mountainside proclaim their weakness in the face of a lapse of time by no means infinite; for no sudden shock could dislodge them and set them falling if they had endured from everlasting, unbruised by all the assault and battery of time.

Last of all, consider this outer envelope which lies above and about the earth and holds it in its embrace. If it is this, as some assert, that generates all things from itself and reclaims them when their days are ended, then it too must consist wholly of matter that is neither birthless nor deathless; for everything that gives of itself to feed the growth of others must thereby be diminished, and be born anew when it reclaims its own.

Here is another line of reasoning. If earth and sky had no

starting-point in time, why have no poets sung of feats before the Theban war and the tragedy of Troy? Why have so many heroic deeds recurrently dropped out of mind and found no shrine in lasting monuments of fame? The answer, I believe, is that *this world is newly made*: its origin is a recent event, not one of remote antiquity. That is why even now some arts are still being perfected: the process of development is still going on. Many improvements have just been introduced in ships. It is no time since organists gave birth to their tuneful harmonies. Yes, and it is not long since the truth about nature was first discovered, and I myself am even now the first who has been found to render this revelation into my native speech.

Alternatively, you may believe that all these things existed before, but that the human race was wiped out by a burst of fiery heat or its cities were laid low by some great upheaval of the world or engulfed by greedy rivers which persistent rains had driven to overflow their banks. All the more reason, then, to concede my point and admit that an end is coming to earth and sky. If the world was indeed shaken by such plagues and perils, then it needs only a more violent shock to make it collapse in universal ruin. There is no clearer proof of our own mortality than the fact that we are subject to the same ailments as those whom nature has already recalled from life.

Again, there can be only three kinds of everlasting objects. The first, owing to the absolute solidity of their substance, can repel blows and let nothing penetrate them so as to unknit their close texture from within. Such are the atoms of matter whose nature I have already demonstrated. The second kind can last for ever because it is immune from blows. Such is empty space, which remains untouched and unaffected by any impact. Last is that which has no available

place surrounding it into which its matter can disperse and
disintegrate. It is for this reason that the sum total of the
universe is everlasting, having no space outside it into which
the matter can escape and no matter that can enter and disintegrate it by the force of impact. But, as I have shown,
the world is not a solid mass of matter, since there is an
admixture of vacuity in things. It is not of the same nature
as vacuity. There is no lack of external bodies to rally out
of infinite space and blast it with a turbulent tornado or
inflict some other mortal disaster. And finally in the depths
of space there is no lack of room into which the walls of
the world may crumble away or collapse under the impact
of some other shock. It follows, then, that the doorway of
death is not barred to sky and sun and earth and the sea's
unfathomed floods. It lies tremendously open and confronts
them with a yawning chasm. So, for this reason, too, you
must acknowledge them to be children of time. For nothing
with a frame of mortal build could have endured from everlasting until now, proof against the stark strength of
immeasurable age.

Consider another possibility. Since civil strife rages
among the world's warring elements on so vast a scale, it
may be that their long battle will some day be decided.
Perhaps the sun and heat will overpower the rivers and
drink their waters dry. They are struggling to do this now,
but have not yet accomplished their aim: the rivers maintain
such ample resources and threaten on their side to deluge
everything from the deep reservoir of the ocean. They, too,
are thwarted: their ranks are thinned by the ocean-scouring
winds and the fiery sun's dissolvent rays, confident of their
power to dry up every drop before the water can achieve
the goal of its enterprise. So these opposing forces maintain
their heated conflict, contending on equal terms for gigantic

issues. But legend tells of one occasion when fire got the upper hand and once when water lorded it over the land.

The victory of fire, when earth felt its withering blast, occurred when the galloping steeds that draw the chariot of the sun swept Phaëthon from the true course, right out of the zone of ether and far over all the lands. Then the Father Almighty, in a fierce gust of anger, struck down the aspiring Phaëthon with a sudden stroke of his thunderbolt, down out of the chariot to the earth. But the sun intercepted the everlasting torch of the firmament in its fall, brought the trembling steeds back to the yoke from their stampede and, guiding them along their proper course, restored the universe to order. Such is the story as recited by the ancient bards of Greece, a story utterly rejected by true doctrine. What may really lead to the triumph of fire is an increase in the accumulation of its particles out of infinite space. Then comes the crisis: either its forces for some reason suffer a setback, or the world shrivels in its parching blasts and comes to an end.

Another legend tells how water likewise once massed its forces and began to prevail, till many cities of men were drowned beneath its floods. Then, when there came some diversion and withdrawal of the reinforcements mustered out of the infinite, the rains halted and the rivers checked their flow.

I will now set out in order *the stages by which the initial concentration of matter laid the foundations of earth and sky*, of the ocean depths and the orbits of sun and moon. Certainly the atoms did not post themselves purposefully in due order by an act of intelligence, nor did they stipulate what movements each should perform. But multitudinous atoms, swept

along in multitudinous courses through infinite time by
mutual clashes and their own weight, have come together
in every possible way and realized everything that could be
formed by their combinations. So it comes about that a
voyage of immense duration, in which they have experienced every variety of movement and conjunction, has at
length brought together those whose sudden encounter normally forms the starting-point of substantial fabrics — earth
and sea and sky and the races of living creatures.

At that time the sun's bright disc was not to be seen here,
soaring aloft and lavishing its light, nor the stars that crowd
the far-flung firmament, nor sea nor sky nor earth nor air
nor anything in the likeness of the things we know — nothing
but a hurricane raging in a newly congregated mass of atoms
of every sort. From their disharmony sprang conflict, which
maintained a turmoil in their interspaces, courses, unions,
thrusts, impacts, collisions and motions, because owing to
their diversity of shape and pattern they could not all remain
in the combinations in which they found themselves or
mutually reconcile their motions. From this medley they
started to sort themselves out, like combining with like,
and to rough out the main features of a world composed of
distinct parts: they began, in fact, to separate the heights of
heaven from the earth, to single out the sea as a receptacle
for water detached from the mass and to set apart the fires
of pure and isolated ether.

In the first place all the particles of earth, because they
were heavy and intertangled, collected in the middle and
took up the undermost stations. The more closely they
cohered and clung together, the more they squeezed out
the atoms that went to the making of sea and stars, sun and
moon and the outer walls of this great world. For all these
are composed of smooth round seeds, much smaller than the

particles of earth. The first element to break out of the earth through the pores in its spongy crust and to shoot up aloft was ether, the generator of fire. Owing to its lightness, it carried off with it a quantity of fire. We may compare a sight we often see when the sun's golden rays glow with the first flush of dawn among the dew-spangled herbage: the lakes and perennial watercourses exhale a vapour, while at times we see the earth itself steaming. It is these vapours, when they all coalesce and combine their substance in the upper air, that weave a cloudy curtain under the sky. Just so in those days the ethereal fire, buoyant and diffusive, coalesced at the circumference and trickled this way and that till it became generally diffused and enveloped the other elements in an ardent embrace.

On this ensued the birth of the sun and moon, whose globes revolve at middle height in the atmosphere. The earth did not claim them for itself, nor did the transcendent ether, because they were neither heavy enough to sink and settle nor light enough to soar in the uppermost zone. Yet in their midway station they are so placed as to revolve actual bodies and to form parts of the world as a whole. Just so in our own bodies, while some members remain fixed at their posts, others are free to move.

When these elements had withdrawn, the earth suddenly caved in, throughout the zone now covered by the blue extent of sea, and flooded the cavity with surging brine. Day by day the encircling ethereal fires and the sun's rays by continual bombardment of the outer crust from every quarter compressed the earth into an ever narrower compass, so that it shrank into itself in its middle reaches and cohered more compactly. So even ampler floods of salty fluid were exuded from its body to swell the billowy plain of ocean. Ever fresh contingents of those particles of heat and air of which I have spoken slipped out to reinforce the sparkling vault of heaven far up above the earth. As the plains settled down, the mountain steeps grew more prominent; for the crags could not sink in, and it was not possible for every part to subside to the same extent.

So the earth by its weight and the coalescing of its substance came to rest. All the sediment of the world, because it was heavy, drifted downwards together and settled at the bottom like dregs. Then sea and air and fiery ether itself were each in turn left unalloyed in their elemental purity, one being lighter than another. Ether, as the clearest and the lightest, floats upon the gusty air and does not mingle its clear substance with the air's tempestuous tumult. It leaves the lower regions to be spun round by eddying whirlwinds, tossed to and fro by veering squalls. It bears its own fires on a steady course as it glides along. The possibility of such a regular and constant flow as this of ether is demonstrated by the Bosporus, a sea which flows with a uniform tide, maintaining perpetually the single tenor of its current.

Let us now take as our theme *the cause of stellar movements*. First, let us suppose that the great globe of sky itself rotates. We must then say that the poles of the celestial sphere are held in place and hemmed in at either extremity by the external pressure of air on both of them. In addition, there must be another current of air, either flowing above in the same direction in which the flashing lights of the ageless firmament revolve, or else moving below in the reverse direction, so that it rotates the sphere on the same principle as we see rivers turning water-wheels by pressure on the scoops.

There remains the alternative possibility that the sky as a

whole is stationary while the shining constellations are in motion. This may happen because swift currents of ether are shut up inside and in their search for an outlet whirl round and round and roll their fires at large across the nocturnal regions of the sky. Or an external current of air from some other quarter may whirl them along in its course. Or they may swim of their own accord, each responsive to the call of its own food, and feed their fiery bodies in the broad pastures of the sky. Which of these possibilities is the truth, so far as this world is concerned, is not easy to establish. But my argument shows what could and may happen throughout the universe in the various worlds formed on various patterns. So I have worked through the list of causes that may produce stellar motions throughout the universe. One of these causes must certainly operate in our world also to speed the march of the constellations. But to lay down which of them it is lies beyond the range of our stumbling progress.

We have now to consider *how the earth remains fixed in the middle of the world*. The answer is that its mass gradually attenuates and dwindles away and that its lower parts are formed of another substance, and this ever since the creation has been combined and united with the airy regions of the world in which it is vitally implanted. That is why it is no burden to the air and does not press down upon it. We know that a man's own limbs, so far as he himself is concerned, have no weight; his head is not a burden to his shoulders, and we do not feel the whole bulk of our bodies pressing down on our feet. But weights of external origin that are laid upon us are burdensome, though often they are much less. The decisive factor is the extent of the power possessed by each particular object. In the same way, the

earth is not a foreign body suddenly introduced and
plumped down upon unfamiliar air. It is a definite part of
the world, conceived simultaneously with it at birth, as we
know our own limbs are with us.

Again, when the earth is suddenly shaken by a sizable
thunderclap, it involves all the atmosphere above it in the
shock. This it could not possibly do if it were not attached
to the airy regions of the world and to the sky. In fact, they
have been linked together and united from the creation and
cling to each other by common roots.

Or consider how all the bulk of our body is upheld by
the flimsy tissue of the spirit, because the two are so closely
interlinked and united. What is it that lifts the body up in
a vigorous jump if not the pervasive spirit which directs the
limbs? Here, then, is evidence of the strength a flimsy
substance can possess when it is united with a massive one,
as the air is with the earth or the human mind with the
human body.

Next, as to *the size of the sun's blazing disc*: it cannot in fact
be either much larger or much smaller than it appears to our
senses. So long as fires are near enough both to transmit
their light and to breathe a warm blast upon our bodies, the
bulk of their flames suffers no loss through distance: the fire
is not visibly diminished. Since, therefore, the heat of the
sun and the light it gives off travel all the way to our senses
and illumine all they touch, its shape and size also must
appear as they really are, with virtually no room for any
lessening or enlargement.

The moon, too, whether it sheds a borrowed light upon
the landscape in its progress or emits a native radiance from
its own body, is not in either case of bulkier dimensions
than those with which it appears to our eyes. For objects

613] COSMOLOGY AND SOCIOLOGY

seen at a distance through a thick screen of air appear
blurred in outline before they are diminished in bulk. It
follows that the moon, which presents a sharp outline and
a precise shape, must appear to us up there just as it is, with
its limits truly defined and in its actual dimensions.

So, too, with every spark of ethereal fire that is visible
from the earth. The magnitude of fires that we see on earth
is very little changed in appearance, one way or the other,
by distance so long as their flickering is still distinct and their
blaze perceptible. This does not exclude the possibility that
the stars may be just a shade smaller than they look or the
least little bit bigger.

How then, if the sun is so small, can it give off such a
flood of light, enough to deluge lands and seas and sky and
permeate the world with a glow of warmth? There is nothing miraculous about this. It is quite possible that from this
one outlet the light of all the world may break out and gush
in an abounding fountain, this being the centre at which
all the atoms of heat forgather from all the world. This
universal confluence then becomes the source from which
the radiance is again dispersed. See how widely a tiny spring
may sometimes water the meadows and inundate the plain.
There is the further possibility that heat issuing from the
relatively small fire of the sun may set the air ablaze, if it
happens that there is air available that is readily kindled by
contact with small emanations of heat. Just so we sometimes
see a general conflagration in corn or stubble started by a
single spark. It may be, again, that round the sun's ruddy
torch, where it flares on high, there extends a wide zone of
fire, charged with invisible heat with no distinguishing
effulgence. Such a zone might add its share to the calorific
energy of the rays.

There is no obvious way of accounting by a simple and straightforward hypothesis for the *movements of the sun* from its summer quarters to its midwinter turning-point of Capricorn and back again upon its tracks to its midsummer limit in Cancer, or of explaining *how the moon is seen to cover in a month the distance on which the sun in its travels spends a full year*. No simple cause, I repeat, can be assigned to these phenomena.

The first possible explanation that suggests itself is that advanced by the revered authority of the great Democritus. On this view, the nearer the heavenly bodies are to the earth, the less are they caught up in the vortex of the heavens. The rushing and impulsive energy of the vortex, it is supposed, fades out and dwindles at lower levels. So the sun, whose path lies far below the ardent constellations, gradually lags behind and drops towards their rear. Much more the moon: the more its lowlier course falls short of the sky and approaches the earth, the less can it keep pace with the stars. The more sluggish the vortex in which it is involved, down here below the sun, the sooner it is overtaken and passed by in the cyclic march by each successive constellation. That is why the moon seems to return more rapidly than the sun to each constellation: it is they in fact that catch up faster on the moon.

Another possibility is that two cross-currents of air blow through the sky, alternating with the seasons: one drives the sun down from the summer constellations towards the ice-bound frigidity of its midwinter turning-point; the other tosses it back out of the cold and dark into the genial region of the torrid stars. So also with the moon and with the planets, which complete great years in orbits as great: we may picture them as blown before winds from alternating quarters. See how the clouds at different levels move in different directions, impelled by conflicting winds. Why should not the heavenly bodies, out in the wide zones of ether, be sped on their several courses by conflicting currents?

The reason why night shrouds the earth in far-flung gloom may be that the sun, exhausted by its long day's journey, has reached the utmost limits of the sky and puffed out its travel-spent fires, enfeebled by excess of air. Alternatively, it may be driven to double back under the earth by the same force that guided its globe above the earth. Correspondingly, when dawn at the determined hour diffuses its rose-red glow through the ethereal regions and flings wide the light of day, it may be that the same sun, which we have pictured as doubling back under the earth, takes possession of the sky with precursive rays and strives to set it ablaze. Or it may be that at the determined hour there is a concentration of fires, a confluence of many particles of heat, which regularly causes the solar radiance to be born anew. So it is related that from the heights of Mount Ida at daybreak scattered fires are seen in the East coalescing as it were into a ball till they form a single sphere. There would be nothing miraculous about such a confluence of fiery particles at such a regularly determined time rebuilding the sun in its splendour. In every department of nature we see a host of phenomena recurring at a determined time. The trees have a set time for blossoming and for shedding their blossoms. At a set time age decrees the shedding of teeth, the growth of a soft down on the downless skin and with it the sprouting of a soft beard from either cheek. Even climatic phenomena – thunderstorms, snow, rain, clouds, winds – do not occur at wholly undetermined seasons of the year. In a world in which the operative causes began in this particular way and phenomena at the outset fell into this pattern, they continue even now to recur consecutively in the same pattern.

As to the lengthening of the day coupled with the shrink-age of night, and the waning of daylight when night is waxing, various views are again tenable. It may be that the same sun traverses unequal arcs of the ethereal sphere below the earth and above, dividing its daily orbit into a greater part and a less. Thus, what it has subtracted from the one half it adds to the opposite one in its revolution, till it comes round to that constellation in which the equinox equates the shades of night with the light of day. At the mid-point of the sun's flight before the north wind and again before the south wind, the sky holds apart the tropics at an equal distance on either side of the sun. This follows from the position of the whole zodiacal belt through which the sun creeps to complete its annual cycle, lighting heaven and earth with radiance cast aslant. Such is the account given by those who have plotted all the regions of the sky and marked the ordered sequence of constellations.

Or it may be that the air in certain regions is denser, so that the flickering glow of fire loiters beneath the earth and cannot easily win through and struggle out to its rising; and that this is why the long winter nights drag on till the advent of day's flashing banner.

Or again, if the truth lies with those who believe that a new sun is caused to rise in a particular quarter by the confluence of fiery particles, it may be that this occurs at varying speeds in alternate seasons of the year.

What, then, of the moon? It may be that it shines only when the sun's rays fall upon it. Then day by day, as it moves away from the sun's orb, it turns more of its illumined surface towards our view till in its rising it gazes down face to face upon the setting sun and beams with lustre at the full. Thereafter, it is bound to hide its light bit by bit

behind it as it glides round heaven towards the solar fire
from the opposite point of the zodiac. Such is the view of
those who picture the moon as a spherical body moving in
an orbit below the sun.

It is equally possible that it rolls round with a lustre of its
own and displays changing shapes of luminosity. For there
may be another body that glides along by its side, masking
and obstructing it in every way but remaining invisible
because it is lustreless.

Or perhaps the moon is a rotating sphere of which one
half is gilded with resplendent light. Then in the course of
its rotation it displays changing shapes, until it turns
towards our wide-eyed gaze that half which is enriched with
fire. Thereafter by the reverse process it veers round and
turns away the luminous half of its rounded globe. Such is
the contention by which the Babylonian lore of the Chal-
daeans strives to confute the art of the astronomers – as
though the theory for which either party fights might not
be true, and there were any reason why you should be more
reluctant to adopt the one than the other.

Lastly, why should not a new moon be created periodically with a definite sequence of determinate shapes? Why
should not each in turn dwindle day by day, and in its place
another be built up to play the same part? It is hard to
formulate any convincing argument that would rule this out
when so many things are created in a definite sequence.
Spring comes, and Venus, and Venus' winged courier Cupid
runs in front. And all along the path that they will tread
dame Flora carpets the trail of Zephyr with a wealth of
blossoms exquisite in hue and fragrance. Next follows
parching heat, hand in hand with dusty Ceres and the north
wind's seasonable blasts. Then autumn steps on the scene,
with Bacchus' revel rout. Soon other seasons follow and

other winds, high thundering from Mount Vultur, ablaze
with southern lightning. To end the pageant, midwinter
brings back its snows and stiffening frost, attended by that
old tooth-chatterer, cold. What wonder, then, if the moon
is born at a set time and again at a set time effaced, when so
many things are created in a definite sequence?

In the same way you must understand that various causes
may account for eclipses of the sun and the moon's occulta-
tions. If the moon can cut off sunlight from the earth, up-
rearing its obstructive head between the two and planting
an unseen sphere in the path of the glowing rays, why should
we not picture the same effect as produced by another body
that glides round for ever lustreless? Or why should not the
sun periodically fail and dim its own fires and afterwards
rekindle its light when it has passed through a stretch of
atmosphere uncongenial to flame, which causes the quench-
ing and quelling of its fire? And again, if the earth in turn
can rob the moon of light by screening off the sun that shines
below while the moon in its monthly round glides through
the clear-cut cone of shadow, why should not some other
body equally well pass under the moon or glide over the
solar orb so as to interrupt the radiant stream of light?
And, supposing that the moon shines by its own lustre, why
should it not grow faint in a determinate quarter of the
heavens while it is passing through a region uncongenial to
its particular light?

I have explained the processes by which the various phenomena may be brought about in the blue expanses of the
firmament. I have made intelligible the forces that may
actuate the movements of the sun and the moon's wander-
ings. I have shown how both may suffer eclipse through the
obscuration of their light and plunge the unexpecting earth

in gloom, as though they blinked and then with reopened eye surveyed the world, aglow with limpid radiance. I return now to the childhood of the world, to consider what fruits the tender fields of earth in youthful parturition first ventured to fling up into the light of day and entrust to the fickle breezes.

First of all, the earth girdled its hills with a green glow of herbage, and over every plain the meadows gleamed with verdure and with bloom. Then trees of every sort were given free rein to join in an eager race for growth into the gusty air. As feathers, fur and bristles are generated at the outset from the bodies of winged and four-footed creatures, so then *the new-born earth first flung up herbs and shrubs. Next in order it engendered the various breeds of mortal creatures*, manifold in mode of origin as in form. The animals cannot have fallen from the sky, and those that live on land cannot have emerged from the briny gulfs. We are left with the conclusion that the name of mother has rightly been bestowed on the earth, since out of the earth everything is born.

Even now multitudes of animals are formed out of the earth with the aid of showers and the sun's genial warmth. So it is not surprising if more and bigger ones took shape and developed in those days, when earth and ether were young. First, the various breeds of winged birds were hatched out of eggs in the spring season, just as now the cicadas in summer crawl out spontaneously from their tubular integuments in quest of sustenance and life. Then it was that the earth brought forth the first mammals. There was a great superfluity of heat and moisture in the soil. So, wherever a suitable spot occurred, there grew up wombs, clinging to the earth by roots. These, when the time was ripe, were burst open by the maturation of the embryos, rejecting moisture now and struggling for air. Then nature directed

towards that spot the pores of the earth, making it open its
veins and exude a juice resembling milk, just as nowadays
every female when she has given birth is filled with sweet
milk because all the flow of nourishment within her is
directed into the breasts. The young were fed by the earth,
clothed by the warmth and bedded by the herbage, which
was then covered with abundance of soft down. The childhood of the world provoked no hard frosts or excessive
heats or winds of boisterous violence. For all things keep
pace in their growth and the attainment of their full
strength. Here then, is further proof that the name of
mother has rightly been bestowed on the earth, since it
brought forth the human race and gave birth at the appointed
season to every beast that runs wild among the high hills and
at the same time to the birds of the air in all their rich
variety.

Then, because there must be an end to such parturition,
the earth ceased to bear, like a woman worn out with age.
For the nature of the world as a whole is altered by age.
Everything must pass through successive phases. Nothing
remains for ever what it was. Everything is on the move.
Everything is transformed by nature and forced into new
paths. One thing, withered by time, decays and dwindles.
Another emerges from ignominy, and waxes strong. So the
nature of the world as a whole is altered by age. The earth
passes through successive phases, so that it can no longer
bear what it could, and it can now what it could not
before.

In those days the earth attempted also to produce a host of
monsters, grotesque in build and aspect – hermaphrodites,
halfway between the sexes yet cut off from either, creatures
bereft of feet or dispossessed of hands, dumb, mouthless

brutes, or eyeless and blind, or disabled by the adhesion of
their limbs to the trunk, so that they could neither do anything nor go anywhere nor keep out of harm's way nor take
what they needed. These and other such *monstrous and mis-
shapen births were created. But all in vain.* Nature debarred
them from increase. They could not gain the coveted flower
of maturity nor procure food nor be coupled by the arts of
Venus. For it is evident that many contributory factors are
essential to the reproduction of a species. First, it must have
a food-supply. Then it must have some channel by which the
procreative seeds can travel outward through the body when
the limbs are relaxed. Then, in order that male and female
may couple, they must have some means of interchanging
their mutual delight.

In those days, again, *many species must have died out altogether*
and failed to reproduce their kind. Every species that you
now see drawing the breath of life has been protected and
preserved from the beginning of the world either by cunning
or by prowess or by speed. In addition, there are many that
survive under human protection because their usefulness has
commended them to our care. The surly breed of lions, for
instance, in their native ferocity have been preserved by
prowess, the fox by cunning and the stag by flight. The dog,
whose loyal heart is alert even in sleep, all beasts of burden
of whatever breed, fleecy sheep and horned cattle, over all
these, my Memmius, man has established his protectorate.
They have gladly escaped from predatory beasts and sought
peace and the lavish meals, procured by no effort of theirs,
with which we recompense their service. But those that
were gifted with none of these natural assets, unable either
to live on their own resources or to make any contribution
to human welfare, in return for which we might let their

race feed in safety under our guardianship – all these, trapped in the toils of their own destiny, were fair game and an easy prey for others, till nature brought their race to extinction.

But *there never were*, nor ever can be, Centaurs – *creatures with a double nature*, combining organs of different origin in a single body so that there may be a balance of power between attributes drawn from two distinct sources. This can be inferred by the dullest wit from these facts. First, a horse reaches its vigorous prime in about three years, a boy far from it: for often even at that age he will fumble in sleep for his mother's suckling breasts. Then, when the horse's limbs are flagging and his mettle is fading with the onset of age and the ebbing of life, then is the very time when the boy is crowned with the flower of youth and his cheeks are clothed with a downy bloom. You need not suppose, therefore, that there can ever be a Centaur, compounded of man and draught-horse, or a Scylla, half sea-monster, with a girdle of mad dogs, or any other such monstrous hybrid between species whose bodies are obviously incompatible. They do not match in their maturing, in gaining strength or in losing it with advancing years. They respond diversely to the flame of Venus. Their habits are discordant. Their senses are not gratified by the same stimuli. You may even see bearded goats battening on hemlock, which to man is deadly poison. Since flame sears and burns the tawny frames of lions no less than any other form of flesh and blood that exists on earth, how could there be a Chimaera with three bodies rolled into one, in front a lion, at the rear a serpent, in the middle the she-goat that her name implies, belching from her jaws a dire flame born of her body? If anyone pretends that such monsters could have been begotten when earth was young and the sky new, pinning his faith merely on that empty word 'young', he is welcome to trot out a string of fairy tales of the same stamp. Let him declare that rivers of gold in those days flowed in profusion over the earth; that the trees bore gems for blossoms, or that a man was born with such a stretch of limbs that he could bestride the high seas and spin the whole firmament around him with his hands. The fact that there were abundant seeds of things in the earth at the time when it first gave birth to living creatures is no indication that beasts could have been created of intermingled shapes with limbs compounded from different species. The growths that even now spring profusely from the soil – the varieties of herbs and cereals and lusty trees – cannot be produced in this composite fashion: each species develops according to its own kind, and they all guard their specific characters in obedience to the laws of nature.

The *human beings* that peopled these fields were far tougher than the men of to-day, as became the offspring of tough earth. They were built on a framework of bigger and solider bones, fastened through their flesh to stout sinews. They were relatively insensitive to heat and cold, to unaccustomed diet and bodily ailments in general. Through many decades of the sun's cyclic course they lived out their lives in the fashion of wild beasts roaming at large. No one spent his strength in guiding the curved plough. No one knew how to cleave the earth with iron, or to plant young saplings in the soil or lop the old branches from tall trees with pruning hooks. Their hearts were well content to accept as a free gift what the sun and showers had given and the earth had produced unsolicited. Often they stayed their hunger among the acorn-laden oaks. Arbutus berries, whose scarlet tint now betrays their winter ripening, were then produced by the earth in plenty and of a larger size. In addition the lusty childhood of the earth yielded a great variety of tough foods, ample for afflicted mortals. Rivers and springs called to them to slake their thirst, as nowadays a clamorous cataract of water, tumbling out of the high hills, summons from far away the thirsty creatures of the wild. They resorted to those woodland sanctuaries of the nymphs, familiar to them in their wandering, from which they knew that trickling streams of water issued to bathe the dripping rocks in a bountiful shower, sprinkled over green moss, and gushed out here and there over the open plain.

They did not know as yet how to enlist the aid of fire, or to make use of skins, or to clothe their bodies with trophies of the chase. They lived in thickets and hillside caves and forests and stowed their rugged limbs among bushes when driven to seek shelter from the lash of wind and rain.

They could have no thought of the common good, no notion of the mutual restraint of morals and laws. The individual, taught only to live and fend for himself, carried off on his own account such prey as fortune brought him. Venus coupled the bodies of lovers in the greenwood. Mutual desire brought them together, or the male's mastering might and overriding lust, or a payment of acorns or arbutus berries or choice pears. Thanks to their surpassing strength of hand and foot, they hunted the woodland beasts by hurling stones and wielding ponderous clubs. They were more than a match for many of them; from a few they took refuge in hiding-places.

When night overtook them, they flung their jungle-bred limbs naked on the earth like bristly boars, and wrapped themselves round with a coverlet of leaves and branches. It is not true that they wandered panic-stricken over the

countryside through the darkness of night, searching with
loud lamentations for the daylight and the sun. In fact they
waited, sunk in quiet sleep, till the sun with his rose-red
torch should bring back radiance to the sky. Accustomed as
they were from infancy to seeing the alternate birth of
darkness and light, they could never have been struck with
amazement or misgiving whether the withdrawal of the sunlight might not plunge the earth in everlasting night. They
were more worried by the peril to which unlucky sleepers
were often exposed from predatory beasts. Turned out of
house and home by the intrusion of a slavering boar or a
burly lion, they would abandon their rocky roofs at dead of
night and yield up their leaf-strewn beds in terror to the
savage visitor.

The proportion of mortal men that relinquished the dear
light of life before it was all spent was not appreciably
higher then than now. Then it more often happened that an
individual victim would furnish living food to a beast of
prey: engulfed in its jaws, he would fill thicket and mountainside and forest with his shrieks, at the sight of his living
flesh entombed in a living sepulchre. Those who saved their
mangled bodies by flight would press trembling palms over
ghastly sores, calling upon death in heart-rending voices,
till life was wrenched from them by racking spasms. In their
ignorance of the treatment that wounds demand, they could
not help themselves. But it never happened then that many
thousands of men following the standards were led to death
on a single day. Never did the ocean levels, lashed into
tumult, hurl ships and men together upon the reefs. Here,
time after time, the sea would rise and vainly vent its fruitless
ineffectual fury, then lightly lay aside its idle threats. The
crafty blandishment of the unruffled deep could not tempt
any man to his undoing with its rippling laughter. Then,

when the mariner's presumptuous art lay still unguessed, it
was lack of food that brought failing limbs at last to death.
Now it is superfluity that proves too much for them. The
men of old, in their ignorance, often served poison to themselves. Now, with greater skill, they administer it to others.

As time went by, men began to build huts and to use
skins and fire. Male and female learnt to live together in a
stable union and to watch over their joint progeny. Then it
was that humanity first began to mellow. Thanks to fire,
their chilly bodies could no longer so easily endure the cold
under the canopy of heaven. Venus subdued brute strength.
Children by their wheedling easily broke down their
parents' stubborn temper. Then neighbours began to form
mutual alliances, wishing neither to do nor to suffer violence
among themselves. They appealed on behalf of their children
and womenfolk, pointing out with gestures and inarticulate
cries that it is right for everyone to pity the weak. It was
not possible to achieve perfect unity of purpose. Yet a
substantial majority kept faith honestly. Otherwise the
entire human race would have been wiped out there and
then instead of being propagated, generation after generation, down to the present day.

As for the various sounds of *spoken language*, it was nature
that drove men to utter these, and practical convenience
that gave a form to the names of objects. We see a similar
process at work when babies are led by their speechless
plight to employ gestures, such as pointing with a finger at
objects in view. For every creature has a sense of the purposes for which he can use his own powers. A bull-calf, before
ever his horns have grown and sprouted from his forehead,
butts and thrusts with them aggressively when his temper is

roused. Panther and lion cubs tussle with paws and jaws when their claws and teeth are scarcely yet in existence. We see every species of winged bird trust in its wings and seek faint-hearted aid from flight. To suppose that someone on some particular occasion allotted names to objects, and that by this means men learnt their first words, is stark madness. Why should we suppose that one man had this power of indicating everything by vocal utterances and emitting the various sounds of speech when others could not do it? Besides, if others had not used such utterances among themselves, from what source was the mental image of its use implanted in him? Whence did this one man derive the power in the first instance of seeing with his mind what he wanted to do? One man could not subdue a greater number and induce them by force to learn his names for things. It is far from easy to convince deaf listeners by any demonstration what needs to be done. They would not endure it or submit for long on any terms to have incomprehensible noises senselessly dinned into their ears.

And what, after all, is so surprising in the notion that the human race, possessed of a vigorous voice and tongue, should indicate objects by various vocal utterances expressive of various feelings? Even dumb cattle and wild beasts utter distinct and various sounds when they are gripped by fear or pain or when joy wells up within them. Indeed we have direct evidence of such distinctions. Molossian hounds, for instance, when first their gaping flabby jowls are drawn back in a grim snarl that bares their hard teeth, give vent to a gruff growl. Very different is the sound when the growl has grown to a loud-mouthed reverberating bay. Different again is the soft crooning with which they fondle their pups when they fall to licking them lovingly with their tongues or toss them with their paws, snapping with open jaws in a playful pretence of gobbling them up with teeth that never close. And different from all these are their howls when left alone in the house, or the whimpering with which they shrink and cringe to avoid the whip. In the same way, when a stallion in the prime of his youth is let loose among the mares, smarting from the prick of winged Cupid's darts, and snorts defiance to his rivals through distended nostrils, his neigh is surely not the same that shakes his limbs on other occasions. So also with the various species of winged birds. The hawks and ospreys and gulls that seek a livelihood among the salt sea-waves all have distinctive cries that show when they are squabbling over their booty or struggling to master a quarry. Some birds even vary their note according to the weather. So the hoarse-throated cawing of long-lived ravens and gregarious rooks varies from time to time according as they are clamouring for showers of rain, as it is said, or summoning wind and storm. If the animals, dumb though they be, are impelled by different feelings to utter different cries, how much the more reason to suppose that men in those days had the power of distinguishing between one thing and another by distinctive utterances!

Here is the answer to another question that you may be putting to yourself. *The agent by which fire was first brought down to earth* and made available to mortal man was lightning. To this source every hearth owes its flames. Think how many things we see ablaze with heaven-sent flame, when a stroke from heaven has endowed them with heat. There is also, however, another possible source. When a branching tree, tossed by the wind, is swaying and surging to and fro and stooping to touch the branches of another tree, the violent friction squeezes out seeds of fire, till sometimes from the rubbing of bough against bough, trunk against trunk, there

flashes out a blazing burst of flame. Either of these occur-
rences may have given fire to mortals. Later it was the sun
that taught them to cook food and soften it by heating on
the flames, since they noticed in roaming through the fields
how many things were subdued and mellowed by the impact
of its ardent rays.

As time went by, men learnt to change their old way of life
by means of fire and other new inventions, instructed by
those of outstanding ability and mental energy. *Kings began to
found cities* and establish citadels for their own safeguard and
refuge. They parcelled out cattle and lands, giving to each
according to his looks, his strength and his ability; for good
looks were highly prized and strength counted for much.
Later came the invention of property and the discovery of
gold, which speedily robbed the strong and the handsome
of their pre-eminence. The man of greater riches finds no
lack of stalwart frames and comely faces to follow in his
train. And yet, if a man would guide his life by true philosophy, he will find ample riches in a modest livelihood
enjoyed with a tranquil mind. Of that little he need never
be beggared. Men craved for fame and power so that their
fortune might rest on a firm foundation and they might live
out a peaceful life in the enjoyment of plenty. An idle
dream. In struggling to gain the pinnacle of power they
beset their own road with perils. And then from the very
peak, as though by a thunderbolt, they are cast down by
envy into a foul abyss of ignominy. For envy, like the
thunderbolt, most often strikes the highest and all that
stands out above the common level. Far better to lead a
quiet life in subjection than to long for sovereign authority
and lordship over kingdoms. So leave them to the blood and
sweat of their wearisome unprofitable struggle along the

narrow pathway of ambition. Since they savour life through another's mouth and choose their target rather by hearsay than by the evidence of their own senses, it avails them now, and will avail them, no more than it has ever done.

So the kings were killed. Down in the dust lay the ancient majesty of thrones, the haughty sceptres. The illustrious emblem of the sovereign head, dabbled in gore and trampled under the feet of the rabble, mourned its high estate. What once was feared too much is now as passionately downtrodden. So the conduct of affairs sank back into the turbid depths of mob-rule, with each man struggling to win dominance and supremacy for himself. Then some men showed how to form a constitution, based on fixed rights and recognized laws. Mankind, worn out by a life of violence and enfeebled by feuds, was the more ready to submit of its own free will to the bondage of laws and institutions. This distaste for a life of violence came naturally to a society in which every individual was ready to gratify his anger by a harsher vengeance than is now tolerated by equitable laws. Ever since then the enjoyment of life's prizes has been tempered by the fear of punishment. A man is enmeshed by his own violence and wrong-doing, which commonly recoil upon their author. It is not easy for one who breaks by his acts the mutual compact of social peace to lead a peaceful and untroubled life. Even if he hides his guilt from gods and men, he must feel a secret misgiving that it will not rest hidden for ever. He cannot forget those oft-told tales of men betraying themselves by words spoken in dreams or delirium that drag out long-buried crimes into the daylight.

Let us now consider why *reverence for the gods* is widespread among the nations. What has crowded their cities with altars and inaugurated those solemn rites that are in vogue to-day in powerful states and busy resorts? What has implanted in mortal hearts that chill of dread which even now rears new temples of the gods the wide world over and packs them on holy days with pious multitudes? The explanation is not far to seek. Already in those early days men had visions when their minds were awake, and more clearly in sleep, of divine figures, dignified in mien and impressive in stature. To these figures they attributed sentience, because they were seen to move their limbs and give voice to lordly utterances appropriate to their stately features and stalwart frames. They further credited them with eternal life, because the substance of their shapes was perpetually renewed and their appearance unchanging and in general because they thought that beings of such strength could not lightly be subdued by any force. They pictured their lot as far superior to that of mortals, because none of them was tormented by the fear of death, and also because in dreams they saw them perform all sorts of miracles without the slightest effort.

Again, men noticed the orderly succession of celestial phenomena and the round of the seasons and were at a loss to account for them. So they took refuge in handing over everything to the gods and making everything dependent on their whim. They chose the sky to be the home and headquarters of the gods because it is through the sky that the moon is seen to tread its cyclic course with day and night and night's ominous constellations and the night-flying torches and soaring flames of the firmament, clouds and sun and rain, snow and wind, lightning and hail, the sudden thunder-crash and the long-drawn intimidating rumble.

Poor humanity, to saddle the gods with such responsibilities and throw in a vindictive temper! What griefs they hatched then for themselves, what festering sores for us, what tears for our posterity! This is not piety, this oft-repeated show of bowing a veiled head before a graven image; this bustling to every altar; this kow-towing and prostration on the ground with palms outspread before the shrines of the gods; this deluging of altars with the blood of beasts; this heaping of vow on vow. True piety lies rather in the power to contemplate the universe with a quiet mind.

When we gaze up at the supernal regions of this mighty world, at the ether poised above, studded with flashing stars, and there comes into our minds the thought of the sun and moon and their migrations, then in hearts already racked by other woes a new anxiety begins to waken and rear up its head. We fall to wondering whether we may not be subject to some unfathomable divine power, which speeds the shining stars along their various tracks. It comes as a shock to our faltering minds to realize how little they know about the world. Had it a birth and a beginning? Is there some limit in time, beyond which its bastions will be unable to endure the strain of jarring motion? Or are they divinely gifted with everlasting surety, so that in their journey through the termless tract of time they can mock the stubborn strength of illimitable age?

Again, who does not feel his mind quailing and his limbs unnerved with shuddering dread of the gods when the parched earth reels at the dire stroke of the thunderbolt and tumult rolls across the breadth of heaven? Do not multitudes quake and nations tremble? Do not proud monarchs flinch, stricken in every limb by terror of the gods and the thought that the time has come when some foul deed or arrogant word must pay its heavy price?

Or picture a storm at sea, the wind scouring the water with hurricane force and some high admiral of the fleet swept before the blast with all his lavish complement of

troops and battle elephants. How he importunes the peace
of the gods with vows! How fervently he prays in his terror
that the winds, too, may be at peace and favouring breezes
blow! But, for all his prayers, the tornado does not relax
its grip, and all too often he is dashed upon the reefs of
death. So irresistibly is human power ground to dust by
some unseen force, which seems to mock at the majestic
rods and ruthless axes of authority and trample on them for
its sport.

Lastly, when the whole earth quakes beneath their feet,
when shaken cities fall in ruins or hang hesitantly tottering,
what wonder if mortal men despise themselves and find a
place in nature for superhuman forces and miraculous
divine powers with supreme control over the universe?

We come next to *the discovery of copper, gold and iron,
weighty silver and serviceable lead*. This occurred when fire
among the high hills had consumed huge forests in its blaze.
The blaze may have been started by a stroke of lightning, or
by men who had employed fire to scare their enemies in
some woodland war, or were tempted by the fertility of the
country to enlarge their rich ploughlands and turn the wilds
into pasturage. Or they may have wished to kill the forest
beasts and profit by their spoils; for hunting by means of
pitfall and fire developed earlier than fencing round a glade
with nets and driving the game with dogs. Let us take it,
then, that for one reason or another, no matter what, a
fierce conflagration, roaring balefully, has devoured a forest
down to the roots and roasted the earth with penetrative
fire. Out of the melted veins there would flow into hollows
on the earth's surface a convergent stream of silver and gold,
copper and lead. Afterwards, when men saw these lying
solidified on the earth and flashing with resplendent colour,

they would be tempted by their attractive lustre and polish to pick them up. They would notice that each lump was moulded into a shape like that of the bed from which it had been lifted. Then it would enter their minds that these substances, when liquefied by heat, could run into any mould or the shape of any object they might desire, and could also be drawn out by hammering into pointed tips of any slenderness and sharpness. Here was a means by which they could equip themselves with weapons, chop down forests, rough-hew timber and plane it into smooth planks and pierce holes in it by boring, punching or drilling. At the outset they would try to do this with silver and gold no less than with tough and stubborn copper. But this would not work. These metals would give under the strain, lacking strength to stand up to such exacting tasks. So copper was more highly prized, and gold with its quickly blunted edge was despised as useless. Now it is copper that is despised, while gold has succeeded to the highest honours. So the circling years bring round reversals of fortune. What once was prized is afterwards held cheap. In its place, something else emerges from ignominy, is daily more and more coveted and, as its merits are detected, blossoms into glory and is acclaimed by mankind with extravagant praises.

At this point, Memmius, you should find it easy to puzzle out for yourself how men discovered the properties of iron. The earliest weapons were hands, nails and teeth. Next came stones and branches wrenched from trees, and fire and flame as soon as these were discovered. Then men learnt to use tough iron and copper. Actually the use of copper was discovered before that of iron, because it is easily handled and in more plentiful supply. With copper they tilled the soil. With copper they whipped up the clashing waves of war, scattered a withering seed of wounds and made a spoil of flocks and fields. Before their armaments all else, naked and unarmed, fell an easy prey. Then by slow degrees the iron sword came to the fore; the bronze sickle fell into disrepute; the ploughman began to cleave the earth with iron, and on the darkling field of battle the odds were made even.

The art of mounting armed on horseback, guiding the steed with reins and keeping the right hand free for action, came earlier than braving the hazards of war in a two-horsed chariot. This again preceded the yoking of two pairs in one harness and the charge of armed warriors in chariots set with scythes. Later the redoubtable snake-handed elephant, its body crowned by a tower, was taught by the men of Carthage to endure the wounds of war and embroil the long-drawn ranks of Mars. So tragic discord gave birth to one invention after another for the intimidation of the nations' fighting men and added daily increments to the horrors of war.

Bulls, too, were enlisted in the service of war, and the experiment was made of launching savage boars against the enemy. Some even tried an advance guard of doughty lions with armed trainers and harsh masters to discipline them and keep them on the lead. But these experiments failed. The savage brutes, enflamed by promiscuous carnage, spread indiscriminate confusion among the cavaliers, as they tossed the terrifying manes upon their heads this way and that. The riders failed to soothe the breasts of their steeds, panic-stricken by the uproar, and direct them with the reins against the enemy. The lionesses hurled their frenzied bodies in a random spring, now leaping full in the face of oncomers, now snatching down unsuspecting victims from behind and dragging them to the ground, mortally wounded in the embrace and gripped fast by tenacious jaws and crooked claws. The bulls tossed their own employers and trampled them underfoot and with their horns gored the flanks and bellies of horses from below and hacked up the very earth with defiant forehead. The infuriated boars with their stout tusks slashed their allies. They reddened with their own blood the weapons broken in their bodies. They mowed down horse and foot pell-mell. The horses would shy away, or rear up and paw the air in a vain attempt to escape the savage onslaught of those tusks. But down you would see them tumble hamstrung, and bury the earth beneath their fallen mass. Even such beasts as their masters had once thought tame enough at home were seen to boil over in the stir of action – wounds, yells, stampedes, panic and turmoil; and none of them would obey the recall. Brutes of every breed were rushing wildly about. The sight must have been just such as is sometimes seen in our own times when elephants, badly wounded by the steel, run wild after turning savagely upon their own associates. If, indeed, the experiment was ever tried. For my part, I find it hard to believe that men had no mental apprehension and pre-vision of this mutual disaster and disgrace before it could happen. It would be safer to assert that this has happened somewhere in the universe, somewhere in the multiplicity of diversely formed worlds, than in any one specific globe. In any event it must have been undertaken more to spite the enemy than with any hope of victory, by men mistrustful of their own numbers and armaments but not afraid to die.

As to *costume*, plaited clothes came before woven ones. Woven fabrics came after iron, because iron is needed for making a loom. Apart from it no material can be made smooth enough for treadles and spindles and shuttles and clattering heddles. Nature ordained that this should be men's work before it was women's. For the male sex as a whole is by far the more skilful and gifted in the arts. But eventually it was damned as effeminate by a censorious peasantry, so that they chose rather to leave it to women's hands while they joined in the endurance of hard labour and by the hardness of their toil hardened hands and thews.

For the *sowing and grafting of plants* the first model was provided by creative nature herself. Berries and acorns, lying below the trees from which they had fallen, were seen to put forth a swarm of shoots in due season. From the same source men learnt to engraft slips in branches and to plant young saplings in the soil of their fields. After that they tried one type of cultivation after another in their treasured plot. They saw the wild fruits grow mild in the ground with cosseting and humouring. Day by day they kept forcing the woodland to creep further up the hillside, surrendering the lower reaches to tillage. Over hill and plain they extended meadowland and cornland, reservoirs and water-courses and laughing vineyards, with the distinctive strip of blue-grey olives running between, rippling over hump and hollow and along the level ground. So the countryside assumed its present aspect of variegated beauty, gaily interspersed with luscious orchards and marked out by encircling hedges of luxuriant trees.

Men learnt to mimic with their mouths the trilling notes of birds long before they were able to enchant the ear by joining together in *tuneful song*. It was the whistling of the breeze through hollow reeds that first taught countryfolk to blow through hollow stalks. After that, by slow degrees, they learnt those plaintive melodies that flow from the flute at the touch of the player's fingers, melodies that took shape far from the busy highways, amid groves and glades and thickets in the solitudes where the shepherd spends his sunlit leisure. These are the tunes that soothed and cheered their hearts after a full meal: for at such times everything is enjoyable. So they would often recline in company on the soft grass by a running stream under the branches of a tall tree and refresh their bodies pleasurably at small expense. Better still if the weather smiled upon them and the season of the year emblazoned the green herbage with flowers. Then was the time for joking and talking and merry laughter. Then was the heyday of the rustic muse. Then light-hearted jollity prompted them to wreathe head and shoulders with garlands twisted of flowers and leaves and dance out of step, moving their limbs clumsily and with clumsy foot stamping on mother earth. This was matter enough for mirth and boisterous laughter. For these arts were still in their youth, with all the charm of novelty.

In the same occupation the wakeful found a means to while away their sleepless hours, pitching their voices high or low through the twisted intricacies of song and running over the pipes with curving lips. This remains a recognized tradition among watchmen to this day, and they have now learnt to keep in tune. But this does not mean that they derive any greater enjoyment from it than did the woodland race sprung from the soil. For what we have here and now, unless we have known something more pleasing in the past, gives the greatest satisfaction and is reckoned the best of its kind. Afterwards the discovery of something new and better blunts and vitiates our enjoyment of the old. So it is that we have lost our taste for acorns. So we have abandoned those couches littered with herbage and heaped with leaves. So the wearing of wild beasts' skins has gone out of fashion.

And yet I daresay that the invention of this costume provoked such envy that its first wearer met his death in an
ambush and the costume itself was so daubed with blood
and torn to shreds by rival claimants that it could not be
used by anyone. Skins yesterday, purple and gold to-day –
such are the baubles that embitter human life with resent-
ment and waste it with war. In this, I do not doubt, the
greater blame rests with us. To the earth-born generation in
their naked state the lack of skins meant real discomfort
through cold; but we are in no way discommoded by going
without robes of purple, brocaded with gold and gorgeously
emblazoned, so long as we have some plebeian wrap to
throw around us. So mankind is perpetually the victim of a
pointless and futile martyrdom, fretting life away in fruitless
worries through failure to realize what limit is set to
acquisition and to the growth of genuine pleasure. It is this
discontent that has driven life steadily onward, out to the
high seas, and has stirred up from the depths the surging
tumultuous tides of war.

It was the sun and moon, the watchmen of the world,
encircling with their light that vast rotating vault, who
taught men that the seasons of the year revolve and that
there is a constant pattern in things and a constant
sequence.

By this time men were living their lives fenced by fortifications and tilling an earth already parcelled out and
allotted. The sea was aflutter with flying sails. Societies
were bound together by compacts and alliances. Poets were
beginning to record history in song. But letters were still a
recent invention. Therefore our age cannot look back to see
what happened before this stage, except in so far as its
traces can be uncovered by reason.

So we find that not only such arts as sea-faring and agriculture, city walls and laws, weapons, roads and clothing, but also without exception the amenities and refinements of life, songs, pictures, and statues, artfully carved and polished, *all were taught gradually by usage* and the active mind's experience as men groped their way forward step by step. So each particular development is brought gradually to the fore by the advance of time, and reason lifts it into the light of day. Men saw one notion after another take shape within their minds until by their arts they scaled the topmost peak.

Book VI

METEOROLOGY AND GEOLOGY

*

IN days of old it was from Athens of high renown that the
knowledge of cereal crops was first disseminated among
suffering mankind. It was Athens that built life on a new
plan and promulgated laws. It was Athens no less that first
gave to life a message of good cheer through the birth of
that man, gifted with no ordinary mind, whose unerring
lips gave utterance to the whole of truth. Even now, when
he is no more, the widespread and long-established fame of
his divine discoveries is exalted to the very skies.

He saw that, practically speaking, all that was wanted to
meet men's vital needs was already at their disposal, and, so
far as could be managed, their livelihood was assured. He
saw some men in the full enjoyment of riches and reputation, dignity and authority, and happy in the fair fame of
their children. Yet, for all that, he found aching hearts in
every home, racked incessantly by pangs the mind was
powerless to assuage and forced to vent themselves in
recalcitrant repining. He concluded that the source of this
illness was the container itself, which infected with its own
malady everything that was collected outside and brought
into it, however beneficial. He arrived at this conclusion
partly because he perceived that the container was cracked
and leaky, so that it could never by any possibility be filled;
partly because he saw it taint whatever it took in with the
taste of its own foulness. Therefore he purged men's breasts

with words of truth. He set bounds to desire and fear.
He demonstrated what is the highest good, after which we
all strive, and pointed the way by which we can win to it,
keeping straight ahead along a narrow track. He revealed
the element of evil inherent in the life of mortals generally,
resulting whether casually or determinately from the
operations of nature and prowling round in various forms.
He showed by what gate it is best to sally out against each
particular form. And he made it clear that, more often
than not, it was quite needlessly that mankind stirred up
stormy waves of disquietude within their breasts.

As children in blank darkness tremble and start at everything, so we in broad daylight are oppressed at times by
fears as baseless as those horrors which children imagine
coming upon them in the dark. This dread and darkness of
the mind cannot be dispelled by the sunbeams, the shining
shafts of day, but only by an understanding of the outward
form and inner workings of nature. The more reason, then,
why I should develop further the argument on which I have
embarked.

I have taught that the sky in all its zones is mortal and its
substance was formed by a process of birth. I have also
elucidated most of the phenomena that occur in the heavens
and that must inevitably occur. Listen now to what still
remains to tell.

Since I have ventured to climb into the lofty chariot of
the Muses, I will explain how the wrath of the winds is
roused and how it is appeased and how all *disturbances of
nature* are allayed when their fury is spent. It is the sight of
these upheavals on earth or in the heavens that frightens
men, when the balance of their minds is upset by fear. It
is this that abases their spirits with terror of the gods and

crushes them cringing on the ground, because ignorance of the causes of phenomena drives them to commit everything to the rule of the gods and to acknowledge their sovereignty. For it may happen that men who have learnt the truth about the care-free existence of the gods fall to wondering by what power the universe is kept going, especially those movements that are seen overhead in the ethereal borderland. Then the poor creatures are plunged back into their old superstitions and saddle themselves with cruel masters whom they believe to be all-powerful. All this because they do not know what can be and what cannot – how a limit is fixed to the power of everything, and an immovable frontier post. Therefore they are the more prone to go astray, misled by blind reasoning. Unless you purge your mind of such notions and banish far away all thoughts unworthy of the gods and foreign to their tranquillity, then the holy beings whom you thus insult will often do you real harm. This is not because the supreme majesty of the gods can in fact be wronged, so as to be tempted in a fit of anger to wreak a savage revenge. No, the fault will be in you. Because you will picture the quiet ones in their untroubled peace as tossed on turbulent waves of anger, you will not approach their temples with a tranquil heart; you will not be able to admit into a breast at peace those images emanating from a holy body that bring to the minds of men their tidings of a form divine. From this you can gather what sort of life must ensue. If this is to be averted from us by true reason, there is still much to add in finely polished verse to the much that I have already delivered. I must get to the root of celestial and terrestrial phenomena. I must sing of storms and the vivid lightning flash, their effects and the causes of their outbreak. Otherwise you may be so scared out of your wits as to map out different quarters of the sky

and speculate from which one the darting fire has come or
into which other it has passed; how it has entered a closed
building, and how after working its will it has slipped out
again.

For this task I invoke your aid, Calliope, most gifted of
the Muses, tranquillizer of men and delight of gods. Point
out my path along the last lap to the predetermined winning-
post, that by your guidance I may earn with eminent
acclaim the victor's crown.

First, then, the reason why the blue expanses of heaven are
shaken by *thunder* is the clashing of clouds soaring high in the
ether, when conflicting winds cause them to collide. A
thunderclap does not issue from a clear stretch of sky: the
normal source of that terrific crash and roll is the point
where the advancing columns of cloud are most densely
serried. Clouds cannot be composed of such dense bodies
as make up stones or logs, nor of such flimsy ones as mist
and drifting smoke. In the one case, they would be forced
to fall like stones by the drag of their dead weight; in the
other, they would be no better able than smoke to cohere
or to contain icy snow and showers of hail. The noise they
make above the levels of the outspread world is comparable
to the intermittent clap of the awning stretched over a large
theatre, when it flaps between poles and cross-beams; or to
the loud crackling, reminiscent of rending paper, that it
makes when riotous winds have ripped it. You can pick out
the former sound in thunder, and you hear it again when
hanging clothes or flying scraps of paper are whipped and
whirled by the wind and swished through the air. At other
times it happens that the clouds cannot so much collide
head-on as pass side by side on different courses, scraping
their bodies together protractedly. That is when our ears

are rubbed by that dry crackling sound, long drawn out, until the clouds have drifted out of close quarters.

Here is another way in which it often seems that a violent burst of thunder has made the whole earth reel and has suddenly cracked and rent apart the ramparts of the all-embracing firmament. A swiftly gathered squall of stormy wind has thrust its way into the clouds. There, being hemmed in, its eddying swirl scoops out an ever-growing hollow walled on every side by cloud with its substance more and more condensed. Finally, the concentrated energy of the wind splits the cloud and explodes it with a nerve-shattering crash. And no wonder, considering that a little bladder full of wind, when suddenly burst, often gives out a similar sound proportionate to its size.

Another cause of the noise emitted by clouds is the wind blowing through them. We often see clouds scudding by profusely branched and jagged; and we all know that when a gale blows through a dense wood, the leaves rustle and the branches rattle. It also happens sometimes that the impetuous power of a strong blast shears through a cloud, smashing it by a frontal assault. What a gale can do up there is clearly shown by its behaviour down here, where it is relatively gentle: even here on earth it bowls over tall trees and hauls them out by the roots.

There are also waves in the clouds – waves that make a booming sound when they break heavily, just as happens in deep rivers and in the wide sea when the surf is breaking.

Another cause of noise is when a blaze of lightning leaps from cloud to cloud. If the receiving cloud is full of water, this promptly quenches the blaze with a loud hiss like the sizzling of red-hot iron fresh from the fiery furnace when we have plunged it straight into cold water. If, on the other hand, the receiving cloud is drier, it immediately catches

fire and burns with a fierce crackling, as when a flame is
swept over laurel-crowned hills by a squall of wind, spreading conflagration in its impetuous advance; for nothing can
compare with Apollo's Delphic laurel in the baleful roar of
crackling flames with which it is consumed.

Lastly, a noise is produced aloft among the mighty clouds
by widespread crumbling of hoar-frost and crashing of hail.
For mountains of storm-rack mingled with hail are packed
together by the compression of the wind and pulverized.

As for *lightning*, it is caused when many seeds of fire have
been squeezed out of clouds by their collision. Just so, if
stone is struck by stone or steel, a light leaps out and
scatters bright sparks of fire. Thunder follows later, when
our ears receive what our eyes saw flashing; for impulses
always travel more slowly to the ears than to sight. You can
test this by watching from a distance a man felling a towering
tree with a two-bladed axe: it so happens that you see the
blow fall before the sound of the stroke reaches your ears.
In the same way we see the lightning before we are aware
of the thunder, which is in fact emitted simultaneously with
the flash from the same cause, being born of the same
collision.

Here is another way in which the clouds bathe the landscape in fleeting brilliance and the lightning is launched
on its quivering flight. When wind has forced its way into a
cloud and, as I explained before, has hollowed and condensed it by eddying round, it becomes heated by its own
movement. You see everything grow fiery hot with motion:
the speed of a long flight even liquefies a leaden sling-bolt.
So then, when this heated wind has burst open a murky
cloud, it scatters seeds of fire pushed out by the force of
the sudden explosion. These cause the zig-zag flashes of

flame. Then follows the noise, which affects our ears more tardily than the visual impulse strikes our eye-balls.

This happens, you must understand, when the clouds are dense and when they are piled high one above another to an amazing altitude. Do not be misled by the fact that to us, gazing from below, the width of the clouds is more conspicuous than the height to which they are built up. Take note when next you get an oblique view of clouds that mimic mountains wafted through the air by the wind, or on some day when all the winds are becalmed you see along a mountain range a motionless mass of clouds heaped upon clouds and weighing them down. Then you will be able to form some notion of their colossal bulk. Then you will see caverns overarched, as it seems, by beetling crags. When squally winds have filled these caverns, they protest clamorously in their cloudy prison with the roar of caged beasts. This way and that they hurl their menacing growls through the clouds. In search of an outlet they prowl round and round. They dislodge seeds of fire from the clouds and roll together a multitude of them. Soon they are spinning a flame within a hollow furnace, till the cloud bursts and out they tumble in a dazzling flash.

Here is yet another reason why that fleeting golden glow of liquid fire leaps down upon the earth. The clouds themselves must contain a great many seeds of fire; for, when they are free from admixture with water, their colour is mostly flame-like and sparkling. Since they must inevitably absorb many such particles from the sunlight, it is natural that they should flush and emit a fiery glow. So, when a driving wind has concentrated and compressed them forcibly in a single spot, they release under pressure those atoms that are the cause of flame-bright flashes.

Lightning may occur also when the clouds in the sky are

thinning out. When the wind gently dissipates and dissolves them in their flight, they must perforce let drop the particles that generate flashes. But at such times the flash is a quiet one, without that appalling accompaniment of crash and rumble.

What, then, of *the nature and composition of thunderbolts?* We may learn from the stricken spots, branded with the mark of heat and the traces of sulphur exhaling noxious fumes. These are signs of fire, not of wind or rain. Besides, they often set fire to buildings and work their will with darting flame in the heart of the house. You must know that this rarefied fire, more than all other fires, is composed by nature of minute and mobile particles to which absolutely nothing can bar the way. So potent is a thunderbolt that it passes through shut rooms like sounds and voices. It passes through stone and metal, and in an instant liquefies bronze and gold. It causes wine to vanish suddenly from unbroken jars, because its heat on arrival easily unknits and rarefies all the surrounding earthenware fabric of the jar, slips nimbly in, separates the atoms of wine and sweeps them away. This, as we see, is more than the sun's heat can accomplish in an age, though never so intense in its radiance. So much more mobile and more masterful is the force of a thunderbolt.

I will now without more ado fulfil my promise to explain to you how thunderbolts originate and how they possess such momentum that their stroke can dismantle towers, demolish buildings, dislodge beams and rafters, uproot and fling down the monuments of the great, rob men of life, butcher cattle pell-mell and wreak all those other forms of mischief that lie within their power.

It must be supposed that thunderbolts originate from

thick and high-piled clouds. They are never really hurled
from the blue, nor from clouds of slight density. This is
unmistakably shown by experience. Indeed, at such times
the air is so crammed with a solid mass of cloud that we
fancy all the darkness has forsaken Hell and come trooping
from every side into the roomy vaults of Heaven. Such is the
ominous night of cloud-rack that gathers overhead, out of
whose gloom the visage of black dread lours down upon us,
when the storm is making ready to launch its bolts. Add to
this that very often out at sea a black tornado falls upon the
waves, like a river of pitch poured out of the sky, charged
with far-shadowing gloom. With its heavy freight of fire
and wind, it trails in its wake a murky tempest big with
levin-bolt and blast. Even on shore men shudder at the sight
and take cover under their roofs. From this we may infer
what a depth of cloud is heaped above our heads. For surely
the earth would not be overcast by such intensity of gloom
were it not that clouds are piled on clouds up and up, till
the sun is blotted out. And surely in their downfall they
would not drench it in such a deluge of rain that rivers
overflow and fields are drowned unless a great bulk of them
were stacked up in the ether.

Here then we have an abundant source of wind and fire,
enough to account for crashes and flashes in plenty. For I
have already shown that hollow clouds contain a great many
particles of heat and necessarily acquire more from the solar
rays and their calorific energy. Therefore, when the same
wind that happens to accumulate them in some one
particular spot has squeezed out many seeds of heat and in so
doing has itself become intermingled with that fire, the
imprisoned eddy spins in a cramped space and there in a
glowing furnace forges a thunderbolt. Two causes combine
to set the whirlwind ablaze, the heat generated by its own

motion and contact with the fire. Then, when the wind is
well aglow and the deadly momentum of the fire has
heightened, the developed thunderbolt suddenly splits the
cloud and out shoots the glancing flame, darting its vivid
blaze across the scene. There follows that shattering roar
that sounds as though the celestial vault had burst asunder
and were crashing down upon our heads. A tremor lays
violent hold upon the earth, and tumult rumbles through
the depth of heaven; for then the whole mass of cloud-rack
is rocked and shaken till it crackles far and wide. After the
shock follows a pelting sluicing shower. It seems as though
the whole ether were transmuted into rain, and the cascade
heralded a return of the universal Deluge – such a cataract
is loosed by the bursting cloud and unpent whirlwind in the
wake of the crashing, darting, devastating fire.

At other times a violent squall of wind impinges exter-
nally upon a cloud already hot with a developed thunderbolt. The wind bursts open the cloud, and out falls that
fiery whirlwind which is what we in our traditional
language term a thunderbolt. This may happen in various
directions according to the direction of the liberating force.

Sometimes again a gust of wind that is fireless at the outset grows fiery in the course of a long flight before it arrives.
It loses on the way certain large atoms, which cannot keep
pace in piercing the air. At the same time it rakes together
out of the air itself and carries along other atoms of tiny
size which commingle in flight so as to form fire. It is in
much the same way that a leaden sling-bolt often grows hot
in its flight through dropping many petrifactive particles and
picking up fire in the air.

Lastly, it may happen that fire is kindled by the sheer
force of the impact when an object is hit by a wind that is
itself cold and fireless. This, of course, is because the shock

343]   METEOROLOGY AND GEOLOGY   227

of the blow causes a conflux of heat atoms both from the
wind itself and from the object that receives the blow.
When we strike stone with steel, out leaps fire: the coldness
of the steel does not prevent atoms of blazing heat from
rushing together at the point of impact. In the same way
an object may be set ablaze by a thunderbolt, provided that
it is suitably inflammable. In any case a strong wind cannot
be absolutely cold, certainly not one launched with such
violence from above. If it is not already ignited *en route*, it
must arrive at any rate warmed through admixture with
heat.

As for the high speed of thunderbolts, the weight of their
impact and the rapidity with which they complete their
hurtling descent, these are due in the first instance to the
accumulation of pent-up energy within the clouds and the
momentum thus acquired. Then, when the cloud can no
longer contain the mounting impetus, the energy is released
and let fly with tremendous drive, like a missile discharged
from a powerful catapult. Add to this that the thunderbolt
is composed of small, smooth atoms. Such a substance is not
easily obstructed by anything. It slips and slides through the
chinks in things and hence does not lose much way on
account of the stoppages caused by collisions. That accounts
for the impetuous onrush of its swooping flight.

Again, while all weights are always possessed of a
natural downward urge, the addition of a push doubles
their speed and enhances their momentum. So the thunderbolt, with its impetus and velocity thus redoubled, dashes
aside whatever may block its advance and hurtles on its way.

Yet again, because it gathers momentum over a long
course, it must acquire ever greater and greater velocity,
which grows as it goes, reinforcing and intensifying the
energy of the impact. It sweeps up all its eddying atoms into

one main current and directs them along a straight course
to a single target. Possibly in its flight it may extract from
the air itself certain particles whose impact stimulates its
own speed.

Through many substances it passes without damaging or
disturbing them, because its fluid fire slips through the gaps.
Through many it forces its way, the atoms of the thunderbolt glancing against the opposing atoms at their points of
interconnexion. It readily dissolves bronze and melts gold
in an instant, because its component atoms, being tiny and
smooth, easily worm their way in and, once in, are quick to
untie every knot and loosen all cohesion.

It is in autumn that the starlit dome of heaven throughout
its breadth and the whole earth are most often rocked by
thunderbolts, and again when the flowery season of spring
is waxing. In cold weather there is a scarcity of fire, and in
hot weather of winds, and then, too, the clouds are not
so thick. So it is in weather between these extremes that the
various causes of the thunderbolt all conspire. Then the
year's turning tide mingles cold and heat, which are both
needed to forge a thunderbolt within a cloud. Then there
may be a clash of opposites, and the air tormented by fire
and wind may surge in tumultuous upheaval. The vanguard
of hot weather is the rear of cold. That is springtime, when
there must accordingly be tussle and turmoil of opposing
forces. Similarly when the retiring heat is embroiled with
the advancing cold in the season we know as autumn, here
again there is a conflict between summer and grim winter.
These then are the year's crises. No wonder if these are the
seasons of abundant thunderbolts; these are the times when
seething tempests rock the sky, engaged as it is on either
hand in the turmoil of a two-fronted fight, on this side
flames, on the other winds and water interfused.

Here then is a plain and intelligible account of the fiery thunderbolt and how it does what it does. It is a fruitless task to unroll the Tuscan scrolls, seeking some revelation of the gods' hidden purpose. That is no way to study from which quarter the darting fire has come or into which other it has passed; how it has entered a closed building, and how after working its will it has slipped out again. If it is really Jupiter and the other gods who rock the flashing frame of heaven with this appalling din and hurl their fire wherever they have a mind, why do they not see to it that those who have perpetrated some abominable outrage are struck by lightning and exhale its flames from a breast transfixed, for a dire warning to mortals? Why, instead, is some man with a conscience clear of any sin shrouded unmeriting in a sheet of flame, trapped and tangled without warning in the fiery storm from heaven? Why do the throwers waste their strength on deserts? Are they getting their hand in and exercising their arms? And why do they allow the Father's weapon to be blunted on the ground? Why does Jupiter himself put up with this, instead of saving it for his enemies? Why, again, does he never hurl his bolt upon the earth and let loose his thunder out of a sky that is wholly blue? Does he wait till clouds have gathered so that he can slip down into them and aim his blows at close range? Why does he launch them into the sea? What is his grudge against the waves and the liquid amplitude of the ocean prairies? If he wants us to beware of the flying bolt, why is he loth to let us see it on its path? If on the other hand he intends the fire to strike us unawares, why does he thunder from the same quarter and so put us on our guard? Why does he herald its coming with darkness and mutterings and rumblings? And how can you believe that he hurls it in several directions at once? Or dare you assert that it never happens that several

strokes are let fly at the same time? In fact it does happen
very often; just as downpours of rain occur simultaneously
in many districts, so it must happen that many thunderbolts
fall simultaneously. Lastly, why does he demolish the holy
shrines of the gods and his own splendid abodes with a
devastating bolt? Why does he smash masterly images of the
gods and rob his own portraits of reverence with a sacrileg-
ious stroke? Why has he a special fondness for high places,
so that we see most traces of his fire on mountain tops?

From what has been said, it is easy to understand what force
flings down into the sea those waterspouts which the Greeks
aptly term *presteres* or 'scorchers'. It sometimes happens that
a sort of pillar descends into the sea as though let down from
above. Around it the waters boil, lashed by madly blowing
blasts, and woe to any ship that is embroiled in this hurly-
burly.

This is sometimes brought about when a prisoned wind
fails to burst a cloud it has possessed but forces it downwards. So it sags down like a pillar lowered into the sea out
of the sky – gradually, like something pushed from above by
a fist at the end of an outthrust arm and so protruding down
into the waves. When the wind has burst this bulge, out it
rushes into the sea and creates a bewildering stir among the
waves. The cloud, in fact, with its elastic structure is forced
down by an eddying whirlwind, which descends with it.
As soon as its teeming bulk has been pushed down to sea-
level, the wind is suddenly let loose into the water and stirs
up all the sea, making it seethe and roar terrifically.

It sometimes happens also that an eddy of wind wraps
itself in clouds through scraping together atoms of cloud
out of the air, and mimics a *prester* let down out of the sky.

When a waterspout drops on dry land and there explodes,

it disgorges a violent vortex of swirling wind. But, since this happens in any case but seldom, and on land our view of it must often be blocked by mountains, the sight is more frequently encountered in the sea's wide prospect under an open expanse of sky.

The *formation of clouds* is due to the sudden coalescence, in the upper reaches of the sky, of many flying atoms of relatively rough material, such that even a slight entanglement clasps them firmly together. The first result is the formation of separate cloudlets. Then these clutch hold of one another and band together. So they grow by mutual fusion and scud before the winds, till the time comes when a raging storm arises.

Notice also what happens on towering mountain peaks. The closer they approach to the sky, the more persistently they steam with a thick obscuring mist of creamy cloud. This is because, when cloudlets are beginning to form but are still too slight to be visible to the eye, they are driven by buoyant winds against the crowning pinnacles of the range. Here the stage is reached in the process of accumulation at which they are sufficiently condensed to become visible, so that they are seen ascending from the summit into the clear sky. As for the prevalence of wind in these upper regions, that is proved by the evidence of our own senses when we climb high mountains.

We must reckon also with the fact that nature causes a constant stream of particles to rise up from the whole ocean, as shown when clothes hung up on the shore receive an accession of moisture. This suggests that the clouds may also be swollen, in no small measure, by an exhalation from the ocean's briny surge; for its moisture is of a kindred quality.

Again, we see vaporous mists ascending from every river and from the land itself. These exudations, wafted up from the earth like breath, mantle the sky with their pall and build up high clouds by gradual coalescence. For they encounter opposing emanations descending from above out of the starry zone of ether, which help them to condense and weave a cloudy curtain under the blue.

Lastly, it happens that atoms composing clouds and storm-rack also come into this sky of ours from outside the world. I have shown that the number of the atoms is numberless and the extent of space infinite, and I have explained with what velocity the atoms fly and how instantaneously they cover an incalculable distance. No wonder, then, if storm and gloom, louring from on high, are often so swift to envelop seas and lands, when through all the corridors of ether on every side – through every pore in the great world's cuticle – the atoms are provided with an outlet and an inlet.

Let me now demonstrate how *rain-drops* condense high up in the clouds and fall to earth in a dripping shower. First, you will not dispute that many atoms of water emanate from every source together with the clouds themselves, and that the clouds and whatever water is in them grow concurrently, just as our bodies grow concurrently with the blood and sweat and any other fluid that exists in our limbs. The clouds also, like dangling fleeces, absorb a lot of sea-water when they are swept by the winds over the wide sea. In the same way moisture is sucked up into the clouds out of every river.

When they are fully charged with many atoms of water amassed in many ways from various sources, the swollen clouds attempt to discharge their freight, and this for two reasons: the force of the wind pushes it out, and the cloud-mass itself, under pressure of increased accumulation, crushes and squeezes from above and makes it ooze out in showers. Again, when clouds are being dissipated by winds or dissolved by the descending impact of the sun's heat, they discharge a drizzle of moisture, just as wax drips freely when melting over a hot fire.

A violent downpour is occasioned when clouds are violently compressed by both forces, accumulation and the assault of wind. Long continuance and persistency of rain occur when a great many atoms of water are in motion, moisture-laden clouds are heaped one on another and come drifting up from every side, and the whole earth exhales a vaporous steam. In this setting, when the sun's rays blazing through the murky reek strike against the droplets of the storm-cloud, then there sparkles out among the black clouds the splendour of the rainbow.

As for the other forms of matter that originate and grow up aloft and condense in the clouds – snow, wind, hail, icy rime and the strong grip of frost that congeals waters and bridles impetuous torrents throughout their course – it is easy enough to discover and picture mentally how one and all come into being or are created, when once you have rightly grasped the properties of the elements.

Learn now *the true nature of earthquakes*. First you must conceive that the earth, in its nether regions as in its upper ones, is everywhere full of windy caves, and bears in its bosom a multitude of meres and gulfs and beetling, precipitous crags. You must also picture that under the earth's back many buried rivers with torrential force roll their waters mingled with sunken rocks. For the plain facts demand that earth should be of the same nature throughout.

With these things lodged and embedded in its bowels, the earth above trembles with the shock of tumbling masses when huge caverns down below have collapsed through age. Whole mountains topple down, and sudden tremors started by that violent shock ripple out far and wide. Naturally enough, when we reflect that whole buildings by the roadside are shaken and jarred by the inconsiderable weight of a wagon and jump in the same way whenever a cobble-stone jolts the iron-shod rims of the wheels on either side. It happens also, when a huge lump is dislodged from the earth by process of time and rolled into vast and roomy gulfs of water, that the wash of the water makes the earth reel and quiver, just as a pot is sometimes unable to stand firm till the water in it has stopped surging to and fro.

Again, when a concentrated wind blowing through subterranean caverns has come to a head and hurls itself with all its might against the lofty vaults, its impulsive pressure tilts back the earth away from its impact. Then houses built up above on the surface – and the more so in proportion as they tower up towards the sky – lean over and bulge out perilously in the same direction, and projecting beams overhang and threaten to crash. And yet men are loath to credit that a day of doom and ultimate catastrophe awaits this mighty world, though they see such a colossal mass of earth heeling over. If there were no backwash of wind, no power would check the downfall of things. As it is, winds bluster and abate alternately, now rallying to the assault, now recoiling from a repulse. So it happens that the earth more often threatens a collapse than executes it. It tilts over and then swings back and after toppling top-heavily recovers its balance. This is how all buildings totter, the top more than the middle, this in turn more than the base and the base hardly at all.

Another cause of the same tremendous quaking is this. When a sudden turbulent squall of wind, whether of external origin or generated within the earth, has rushed into the subterranean hollows, it first rages there tumultuously among the vast caverns, swirling and eddying. Then, with intensified energy, it forces its way out and, splitting open the earth from its depths, creates a stupendous chasm. This is what happened in Syrian Sidon and at Aegium in the Peloponnese, when these cities were demolished by such an outrush of wind and the resulting earthquake. Many other towns have been laid low by mighty earthquakes on dry land, and many cities with their citizens have been engulfed in the sea. If the wind does not break out, the fury of its accumulated momentum is dissipated through a multitude of underground passages as a passing shudder that sets the earth trembling. It behaves in fact just like the cold air that penetrates our limbs and makes us shiver and shake in spite of ourselves.

So through the menaced cities men tremble with a two-edged terror. While they dread the roofs above, they are afraid that the earth may suddenly fling open its caverns below, gaping wide to reveal a yawning chasm which it will fill pell-mell with its own wreckage. Let them go on imagining that sky and earth are indestructible and destined to life everlasting. From time to time the visible presence of peril stabs them in one quarter or another with a secret qualm of fear that the earth may suddenly be whisked away from under their feet into the abyss and, robbed of its foundation, the whole world in a wild chaotic welter may follow it to perdition.

A point that sometimes occasions surprise is *why nature does not cause the sea to grow bigger*, considering what a huge influx of water it receives from all the rivers that flow into it from every side. Add to these the stray showers and flying rain-storms by which every sea and every land is drenched and douched. Add the sea's own springs. And yet, compared to the total bulk of the ocean, all these together scarcely amount to a single drop. This makes it less remarkable that the vast ocean does not grow still vaster. Besides, a large proportion of this increase is subtracted by the heat of the sun. We see how dripping wet clothes are dried by the sun's parching rays. We see, too, that the oceans exposed to them are multitudinous and of huge extent. However small the quantity that the sun may absorb from the sea at any parti-cular point, yet over such an expanse the total loss will be considerable. Then, again, the winds that scour the ocean may carry off a good deal of moisture, since we often see roadways dried up by the winds in a single night and soft mud hardened to a crust. Again, I have shown that the clouds too pick up a lot of moisture drawn from the wide ocean levels and sprinkle it over all the earth when it is raining above the land and the clouds are blown along by the winds. Lastly, the earth is of an open texture and is contiguous with the sea, encircling its shores on every side. Therefore, just as water enters the sea from the land, so it must trickle into the land out of the briny gulf. The brine is filtered out, and the main bulk of the water flows back to reassemble in full at the fountainhead. Hence it flows overground, a steady column of sweet fluid marching down the highway already hewn with liquid foot for the guidance of its waves.

I will now explain how it happens that flames sometimes shoot out in such a tornado through the throats of *Mount Etna*. For it was no light matter when the fiery storm exerted its despotic power over the fields of Sicily. The eyes of neighbouring nations were drawn towards it, when they saw the smoky flare spread over every quarter of the sky. Their hearts were filled with dreadful apprehension that nature might be planning some revolutionary change.

This is a problem that calls for wide and deep contemplation and far-ranging survey. You must remember that the universe is fathomless, and reflect how minute a part of the whole is one world – an infinitesimal fraction, less in proportion than one man compared to the whole earth. If you look squarely at this fact and keep it clearly before your eyes, many things will cease to strike you as miraculous. Does anyone think it a miracle if somebody catches a fever that enflames his body, or is racked throughout his frame by a painful disease? A foot suddenly begins to swell. Sometimes a stab of anguish lays hold of the teeth or pierces right into the eyes. A fiery rash erupts and worms its way through the body, burning every part it occupies as it crawls from limb to limb. All this because there is a multiplicity of atoms, and this earth and sky of ours have plagues in plenty to generate a superabundance of disease. In just the same way we must picture this earth and sky as amply supplied out of the infinite with matter to jolt the earth with a sudden shock, to set a wild tornado racing over sea and land, to make the fires of Etna erupt and the sky burst into flame. For this too happens: the heavenly regions actually blaze. And rainstorms of abnormal intensity are similarly due to such casual concentrations of water atoms. Do you think the tumultuous burst of conflagration too huge for such an origin? Why, any river seems huge to one who has never seen a bigger. So does a tree or a man. The largest thing a man has seen of any sort strikes him as huge, whereas all of them together, with sky and earth and sea thrown in, are nothing to the sum total of the universe.

I will now turn to the specific question, by what means that suddenly quickened flame spouts from the stupendous furnaces of Etna. First, then, the whole interior of the mountain is hollow, honeycombed with basaltic caverns. Next, in all the caves there is air and wind, the wind being produced by disturbance of the air. When this has been thoroughly heated and in its raging has heated the surrounding rocks and earth where it comes in contact and extracted their content of fire ablaze with leaping flames, it wells up and flings itself skyward by the direct route of the gaping throat. So it scatters fire and ashes far and wide, rolling dense clouds of murky smoke and discharging boulders of staggering weight. There can be no doubting that this is the work of wind at its most tempestuous.

Furthermore, along one extensive stretch the sea dashes its waves against the roots of this mountain and sucks back the undertow. From this sea subterranean caverns penetrate all the way to the depths of its throat. It cannot be doubted that by this channel a blend of wind and water from the open sea is forced into the heart of the mountain. From here it spouts out, shooting up flame, volleying stones and disgorging clouds of sand. For at the very summit there are *craters* or 'mixing bowls', as the Sicilians call them, which we term 'throats' or 'mouths'.

There are some *phenomena to which it is not enough to assign one cause:* we must enumerate several, though in fact there is only one. Suppose you were to see the lifeless body of a man lying some distance away. You would have to mention all the possible causes of his death to be sure of mentioning the right one. You could not prove that he had perished by the sword or by cold, by sickness or by poison. But we know that whatever has happened to him must fall into one category of this sort. And there are many other questions that we are obliged to answer in the same way.

The Nile, for instance, unlike any other river on earth, rises on the threshold of summer and floods the fields of all Egypt. The reason why it normally irrigates Egypt at the height of the heat may be because in summer there are north winds blowing against its mouths – the winds that are said to be *Etesian* or 'seasonal' at that time. These winds, blowing against the stream, arrest its flow. By piling up the water they raise its level and hold up its advance. There is no doubt that these breezes do run counter to the river. They blow from the cold stars of the Pole. The Nile, on the other hand, comes out of the torrid south, rising in the heart of the noonday region among races of men whose skin is burnt black.

It is also possible that a great sand-bar is heaped against the river mouths in opposition to the current when the wind-swept sea drives the sand shoreward. In this way the river has less freedom of egress, and the downflow of its current loses momentum.

Or again, it is possible that at this season heavier rains fall near its source, because then the Etesian blasts from the north concentrate all the clouds in those parts. It may be assumed that, when these southward-driven clouds have massed in the noonday region, they are eventually accumulated there and squeezed against high mountains.

Lastly, it may be that a spate of water forms in the heart of the Ethiopian highlands when gleaming snows are forced to flow down into the plains by the liquefying beams of the all-irradiating sun.

Let me now explain the nature of those *lakes and such like that are called Avernian.* First they owe the name Avernus (or *Aornos*) to the fact that they are inimical to all birds: when the line of their flight has brought them over such places, they rest on their oars, furl their plumy sails and tumble headlong with nerveless necks outstretched. So they fall to earth, if the lie of the land so determines, or into the water, if it be a lake of Avernus that lies outspread below them. There is such a spot near Cumae, where hills give off an acrid fume of sulphur, fed by hot springs. There is another within the walls of Athens, on the very crest of the Acropolis, by the temple of the beneficent virgin Pallas Athene, to which cawing crows never wing their bodies, no matter how the altars smoke with burnt offerings. Not that they are really in such dread of Pallas' dire displeasure, which they had brought on them by their prying, as Grecian bards have sung; but the nature of the place produces this effect spontaneously. In Syria, too, there is said to be a spot that evidently possesses a similar property, affecting even quadrupeds: as soon as they set foot within it, the potency of the place causes them to fall down flat, as though they were suddenly sacrificed to the Powers Below.

All these phenomena occur in the course of nature, and the causes from which they spring are plain to see. There is no need to imagine that such places are gateways to Hell, or indulge in the further fancy that by this route spirits are drawn into the Infernal Regions by the Powers Below, as lightfooted stags are commonly supposed to draw serpents from their lairs by the breath of their nostrils. How far this is from reality you may now learn, for I am setting out to give you the true explanation.

I will begin by repeating what I have often said before, that in the earth there are atoms of every kind. Many of them, those that serve as food, have vitalizing powers;

many are such as to instil disease and hasten death. I have already shown that substances vary in their power to promote life in various living species, owing to differences in their nature and structure and their atomic shapes. Many hurtful particles enter through the ears; many noxious and prickly ones slip in through the nostrils, and not a few are to be avoided by the sense of touch or shunned by sight, or are disagreeable to taste.

Next, it is plain to see how many things in their action on human senses are intensely nauseating and noisome. Certain trees are possessed of a shade so oppressive that they often provoke a headache in one who lies outstretched on the grass beneath them. Among the high hills of Helicon there is even a tree with the property of killing a man by the baleful scent of its blossom. Obviously, the reason why all these grow out of the soil is because the earth contains many seeds of many things mixed together in many ways and delivers them separately.

Again, when a night lamp, newly extinguished, assails the nostrils with its pungent reek, an epileptic prone to fits of foaming and falling is overcome with drowsiness. The heavy scent of beaver musk makes a woman droop in slumber and the gay broidery slip from her dainty hands, if she smells it at the time of menstruation. And there are many other things that enervate and slacken the thews throughout the body and unsettle the vital spirit in its inmost recesses.

Again, if you loiter too long in a hot bath after a heavy meal, how easily it often happens that you collapse on the middle of the seat among the steaming water. How easily the drowsy fume and scent of charcoal passes into the brain, unless we have taken water beforehand. When parching fever has laid hold of the limbs, then the scent of wine is like a knock-out blow.

In the earth itself you often see sulphur generated and malodorous asphalt congealing. When men are following veins of gold and silver, groping with their picks in the bowels of the earth, what fumes are emitted from the pits of Scapte Hyle! What malignant breath is exhaled by gold mines! How it acts upon men's features and complexions! Have you not seen or heard how speedily men die and how their vital forces fail when they are driven by dire necessity to endure such work? All these vapours, then, are given off by the earth and blown out into the open, into the unconfined spaces of the air.

So also these Avernian places must send up an effluence deadly to birds on the wing. As this rises from the earth into the winds, it poisons a certain tract of air. No sooner has a bird winged its way into this tract than it is caught and halted by the invisible venom. Down it tumbles in a sheer fall on the very course in which the vapour rises. Once it has fallen here, the action of the same vapour expels the remnants of life from all its limbs. The first reaction, of course, is a sort of vertigo. Then, when they have fallen into the very fountainhead of the poison, they can do nothing there but cough up life itself, enveloped as they are in a cloud of the deadly stuff.

It also happens sometimes that this effluence from Avernus dispels all the air that lies between the birds and the earth, so that this space is left almost void. When their flight has brought them straight into such a place, the upthrust of their pinions is forthwith lamed and baffled, and all the efforts of either wing are nullified. Since they can no longer support themselves by resting on their wings, nature of course compels them to drop to earth by their own weight. Lying in the midst of almost total vacuity, they dissipate their vital spirits through all the pores of the body.

Let us now consider *why it is that well water is warmer in winter and cooler in summer*. This happens because in summer the earth is relaxed by the warmth and any particles it may contain of its own heat are dispersed into the air. The more the earth is drained of heat, the colder grows the water embedded in it. Conversely, when all the earth is compressed by cold and contracts and virtually congeals, it naturally happens that in contracting it squeezes out any heat it may contain into the wells.

It is said that next the temple of Egyptian Amon there is a spring that is cold through the daylight hours but warm at night. By this spring men are unduly impressed. Some suppose that it catches heat from the sun's ardour below the earth, when night has shrouded the lands in dreadful darkness. This theory is very wide of the mark. When water cannot be warmed from above by the sun's touch on its naked body, for all the blazing incandescence of the uplifted luminary, how can the same sun bake through the solid substance of earth from beneath so as to imbue the same water with a glow of warmth? Why, the sun with its fiery rays can scarcely gain admission for its heat into a shuttered house. What then is the explanation? Evidently the earth surrounding the spring is of looser texture than other earth, and there are many particles of fire near the body of water. When the dewy waves of night flow over the earth, the soil is immediately chilled through and condensed. So it happens that, as if it were squeezed in the hand, it forces out into the spring all the particles of fire it contains; and it is these that make the water warm to touch and steamy. Then, when the risen sun has loosened and relaxed the earth with the interpenetrating heat of its rays, the atoms of fire return to their former positions and all the warmth of the water passes into the earth. That is why the spring is cool by daylight. Besides, the spring-water exposed to the impact of sunbeams is rarefied at daybreak by the pulsating radiance. This causes it to lose all the particles of heat it possesses, just as water often loses its content of frost and dissolves its ice and looses its bondage.

There is also a certain cold spring such that a piece of tow placed above it is normally quick to catch fire and burst into flame. Similarly, a torch floating in its waters is set alight and blazes wherever the breezes drift it. The reason obviously is this. There are in the water a great many atoms of heat; and particles of fire must rise out of the depths of the earth all the way through the spring and so escape by exhalation into the air. There are not, however, so many of them as to heat the spring. Besides they are forcibly impelled to burst out suddenly through the water disconnected and unite on the surface. We may compare that spring of fresh water at Aradus, which wells up in the sea and dispels the salty waves that surround it, and those many other places where the sea provides a welcome refreshment to thirsty mariners by spouting out fresh water amongst the salt. So in this spring the fiery atoms may well up and spout out. When they cluster together on the tow or cling to the substance of the torch, they readily catch fire there and then, because tow and torch also contain many seeds of hidden fire. You must have noticed, again, how a newly extinguished wick, when you bring it near to a night-burning lamp, catches light before it has touched the flame. A torch behaves in the same way. And many things besides are kindled at a distance by mere contact with heat before they are actually dipped in the fire. This, then, is what we must picture as happening also in this spring.

At this point, I will set out to explain what law of nature

causes iron to be attracted by that stone which the Greeks call from its place of origin *magnet*, because it occurs in the territory of the Magnesians. Men look upon this stone as miraculous. They are amazed to see it form a chain of little rings hanging from it. Sometimes you may see as many as five or more in pendent succession swaying in the light puffs of air; one hangs from another, clinging to it underneath, and one derives from another the cohesive force of the stone. Such is the permeative power of this force.

In matters of this sort it is necessary to establish a number of facts before you can offer an explanation of them. This may mean approaching the problem by a very roundabout route. For this reason I beg you to lend me your ears and your mind with particular attentiveness.

In the first place, it must be a fact that all visible objects emit a perpetual stream and shower of particles that strike upon the eyes and provoke sight. From certain objects there also flows a perpetual stream of odour, as coolness flows from rivers, heat from the sun, and from the ocean waves a spray that eats away walls round the seashore. Sounds of every sort are surging incessantly through the air. When we walk by the seaside, a salty tang of brine commonly enters our mouth; when we watch a draught of wormwood being mixed in our presence, a bitter effluence touches it. So from every object flows a multiform stream of matter, rippling out in all directions. The stream must flow without rest or intermission, since our senses are perpetually alert and everything is always liable to be seen or smelt or to provoke sensation by sound.

Let me now re-emphasize, what is made crystal-clear in my first book, the extreme looseness of the structure of all objects. A knowledge of this fact is relevant to many problems. In tackling the problem with which I am now confronted, it is especially necessary to establish that there is no perceptible object that does not consist of a mixture of matter and vacuity. In the first place, we find that in caves the rocky roofs exude moisture and drip with trickling drops. Similarly in our own bodies sweat oozes from every surface; hairs grow on the chin and on every limb and member; food is diffused through every vein, building and sustaining the most outlying parts even to the nails. So also, when we hold full drinking vessels, we feel that cold and heat pass through bronze and through gold and silver. The stone partitions of houses are pervious to voices and to scent and cold and the heat of fire, which penetrates also through hard iron. Even the cuirass of sky, which encompasses the world, is not proof against the invasion of tempest and pestilence from without. Storms that are born of earth are duly allayed by absorption into the sky; and those of celestial origin into the earth. In short, nothing exists but amalgams of matter and space.

Add to this that not all the particles thrown off by objects are identical in their effect on the senses or on particular substances. The sun bakes and parches earth; but it melts ice, and its rays cause deep drifts of snow on the high hills to thaw. Wax, too, is liquefied by exposure to its heat. Similarly, fire liquefies bronze and melts gold; but it shrivels skins and flesh and makes them shrink. Water hardens iron coming fresh from the fire; but it softens skins and flesh that heat has hardened. To bearded goats wild olive is as delicious as if it were redolent of ambrosia and steeped in authentic nectar; yet to man there is no plant whose foliage is more unpalatable. Pigs fight shy of marjoram and shrink from perfume in general; what seems to us on occasion a welcome restorative is dire poison to their bristly bodies. On the other hand filth that nauseates and revolts us

is evidently delectable to pigs, so that they are never weary
of wallowing in it from head to tail.

There is one more point that clearly ought to be made
before I embark on the matter in hand. The innumerable
interstices that occur in different objects must be possessed
of mutually dissimilar natures, each having its own peculia-
rities and its own system of passage-ways. In living creatures,
for instance, there are various senses, each of which affords
an entry for its own specific object. We see that sounds
penetrate into one organ of sense, the savour of juices into
another, the odour of an exhalation into a third. It is evident
too that one thing seeps through stone, another through
wood, another through gold, while yet another leaks
through silver or glass. One medium is pervious to sight,
another to heat. The same medium is traversed by different
elements at different speeds. This, of course, results
inevitably from the great diversity, to which we have just
alluded, in the nature of their internal passage-ways, due to
differences in the nature and texture of substances.

So much by way of preface, to posit and establish the
necessary premisses for our argument. On this basis it will
be easy to elucidate the problem and lay bare the whole
cause of the attraction of iron. First, this stone must emit
a dense stream or emanation of atoms, which dispels by a
process of bombardment all the air that lies between the
stone and the iron. When this space is emptied and a large
tract in the middle is left void, then atoms of the iron all
tangled together immediately slide and tumble into the
vacuum. The consequence is that the ring itself follows and
so moves in with its whole mass. No other substance is so
rigidly held together by the intertanglement of its elemental
atoms as cold iron, that stubborn and benumbing metal.
No wonder, then, since the impulse comes from the atoms,

if a cluster of particles from the iron cannot drop into the void without the whole ring following. This it does, and continues to follow till it actually reaches the stone and clings to it by invisible ties. This happens in any direction in which there is a vacuum, whether the immediately adjoining particles move into it sideways or upwards. Of course they cannot rise up into the air of their own accord; but they are impelled by blows from other quarters.

The process is facilitated and the movement helped on by a contributory cause: as soon as the air in front of the ring is rarefied and the space fairly well emptied and evacuated, it thereupon happens that all the air situated at the back of the ring pushes and shoves it forward from behind. For objects are always being pelted by the surrounding air; but in this case it happens that the iron is pushed by the pelting because in one direction there is a vacuum ready to receive it. This air of which I am speaking creeps nimbly in through the many porosities in the iron and comes up against its tiny particles so as to push and drive it along as sails and ship are driven by the wind.

Again, all objects must contain air within their bodies, since all are of loose texture and all are encompassed and bounded by air. Accordingly the air that lies hidden in the core of the iron is perpetually surging to and fro in a restless motion. By this means, no doubt, it keeps on battering the ring and unsettling it from within. And by the same means the ring is, of course, kept moving in the direction in which it has once launched itself by its plunge into the vacuum.

It also happens at times that iron moves away from this stone; its tendency is to flee and to pursue by turns. I have even seen Samothracian rings of gilded iron jump up and iron filings grow restive inside copper cups when this magnet stone was put under them. So eager, it seemed, was the iron to run from the stone. The reason why the inter-position of copper causes such a turmoil is doubtless this. After the effluence of the copper has first taken possession of the open passage-ways in the iron and occupied them, along comes the effluence of the magnet and finds every-thing full in the iron and so has no way of passing through as before. It is therefore compelled to pelt and batter the texture of the iron with its stream. In this way it repels the iron from itself and through the copper it drives away what otherwise it normally attracts.

There is no need to be surprised that the effluence from this stone has no power to impart a similar motion to other substances besides iron. Some are held fast by their weight, for instance, gold. Others cannot be moved anywhere, because their loose texture allows the effluence to pass through intact; a clear example of this class is wood. Iron, which by its nature lies midway between the two, needs only the addition of some particles of copper and then it yields to the current from the Magnesian stones.

These phenomena are not so different from others that I cannot find plenty of parallels to adduce, in which a unique relation exists between two substances. First, you see that stones are held together only by mortar. Wood, on the other hand, can be joined only by means of bulls' glue; and then it more often happens that cracks in boards gape open through a natural flaw than that the glutinous cement relaxes its grip. The juices of the vine will mix with spring-water when ponderous pitch and buoyant olive oil refuse. The purple dye of the murex combines only with wool, and that so firmly that it can never be parted: not though you should labour with Neptune's flood to resolve it; not though all the ocean with all its waves essayed to cleanse it. Again, is there not one thing only that will weld gold to gold? Is not copper soldered to copper by nothing but tin? How many other examples might be found! But to what purpose? There is no need for you to follow such a round-about route to your goal, nor for me to expend such labour on the point. Better to sum up a long argument in a few brief words. When the textures of two substances are mutually contrary, so that hollows in the one correspond to projections in the other and *vice versâ*, then connexion between them is most perfect. It is even possible for some things to be coupled together, as though interlinked by hooks and eyes. And such, it would rather seem, is the linkage between iron and magnet.

I will now explain *the nature of epidemics* and the source from which the accumulated power of pestilence is able to spring a sudden devastating plague upon the tribes of men and beasts. In the first place, I have shown above that there are certain atoms of many substances that are vital to us, and that on the other hand there must be countless others flying about that are pestiferous and poisonous. When these, by some chance, have accumulated and upset the balance of the atmosphere, the air grows pestiferous. This crop of pesti-lence and plague either comes in through the sky from out-side, like clouds and mists, or very often springs from the earth itself when it has been rotted by drenching with unseasonable rains and pelting with sunbeams.

You should note also how unaccustomed climates and waters affect those who venture far from home and country because of the wide range of variation in things. How else are we to account for the difference between the climate that prevails among the Britons and that of Egypt, where the celestial axis is tilted askew, or between the Crimea and Cadiz and right on to the land where the skins of men are

burnt black? As we see these four regions mutually distinguished by the four winds and quarters of the sky, so their
inhabitants are markedly distinct in complexion and
features and in their susceptibility to particular diseases.
There is elephantiasis, for instance, which is bred in the
heart of Egypt on the banks of the Nile and nowhere else.
In Attica the feet are attacked by gout; in Achaia it is the
eyes that suffer. To other members and organs other regions
are adverse. This is brought about by variations in the air.

Let us suppose, then, that some atmosphere that chances
to be uncongenial to us is set in motion. The baleful air
begins to creep. Like mist and cloud it glides and, wherever
it comes, it sows disorder and change. When at length it
makes its way into our region, it contaminates the atmosphere there, making it conformable to itself and unfriendly
to us. So, without warning, this new plague and pestilence
either falls upon the water or settles right on the growing
wheat or on other human food or pasturage of animals; or
else it remains suspended in the air itself so that, when we
inhale the polluted atmosphere, we cannot help absorbing
these foreign elements into our system. It is in much the
same way that a plague often falls on cattle or a murrain on
bleating sheep already enfeebled. It makes no odds whether
it is we who move into unpropitious regions and change the
atmospheric garment that enwraps us or whether nature
brings to us an uncongenial atmosphere, or something else
to which we are unaccustomed, to menace us with the
advent of the unfamiliar.

Of this nature was the fatal tide of pestilence that once
laid waste the Athenian fields, turning the highways into
deserts and draining the city of citizens. From its well-
spring in the heart of Egypt it traversed a wide expanse of
air and billowy plains and swooped at length upon all the

Attic folk. Then they began to surrender, battalions at a time, to sickness and death. First they would find their heads enflamed with feverish heat and their eyes bright with a bloodshot flush. Then the throat would turn black and sweat internally with blood; the pathway of the voice became blocked and constricted by ulcers; the tongue, the mind's interpreter, enfeebled by pain, grew troublesome to move and rough to touch and began to ooze blood. Then, when the malady passing down the throat had filled the victim's chest and flowed into his distressful heart – then indeed all the bastions of life began to totter. His breath began to emit through the mouth a foul odour like the stench that rises from carcases thrown out to rot. The vigour of the mind as a whole and all the body began to wilt, now on the very threshold of death. The intolerable sufferings were unremittingly attended by racking pain and outcries blent with groans. The sufferers were shaken night and day by incessant retching that convulsed every limb and sinew and, weary as they were already, wore them down with exhaustion.

You would not observe any excessive heat in the surface regions of the body; rather, it felt tepid to the touch of the hands. At the same time the whole body reddened, as though scarred with ulcers. It looked as though every limb were inflamed with a spreading fire of erysipelas. But the inward parts of the victims were ablaze to the very bones. A flame was blazing in their stomach as though in a furnace. It was no good applying anything, however light or flimsy, to their limbs, except continual cooling and ventilation. Some of the sufferers would immerse their fevered limbs in chilly streams, flinging their bodies naked into the waves. Many hurled themselves headlong down from a height into the water of a well, their mouths gaping wide before they got there. The quenchless parching thirst in which their bodies were steeped made a thorough drenching no more satisfying than a few driblets.

There was never any easing of the strain. The body lay exhausted. The attendants by the sick bed hushed their voices in unspoken fear. But still those staring eyes, hot with fever, followed every movement and never closed in sleep.

Then many signs of death began to appear: the mind delirious with agony and terror; the brow contracted; the features wrung with frenzy and passion; the ears tormented by incessant noises; the breath coming in short gasps, or heavy and laboured: a glistening stream of sweat trickling down the neck; a thin phlegm in little drops, tinged with yellow and tasting of salt, painfully ejected from the throat by a hoarse cough. The sinews of the hands began to twitch, the limbs to tremble, and from the feet a persistent chill spread very gradually upwards. Then the last hour drew on, heralded by pinched nostrils, the tip of the nose narrowed to a point, hollow eyes, sunken temples, skin cold and hard, lips parted and drooping, forehead bulging and distended. After this it was not long before the limbs stiffened in death. About the eighth kindling, or the ninth, of the sun's diurnal torch they gave up the ghost.

If the victim, as might happen, stopped short of this fatal extremity, before long by way of loathsome ulcers and a black flux from the bowels he was overtaken none the less by a lingering death. Or else, in many cases, he was seized by a flow of putrid blood through choked nostrils accompanied by a violent headache, and through this channel all the strength of his body ebbed away.

If he survived this malignant efflux of foul blood, the disease had still to make its way into his joints and sinews and right into the organs of generation. Some in their overwhelming dread of death saved their lives by castration. Others stayed alive after a fashion minus hands and feet or with the loss of their eyesight: so completely were they mastered by the dire dread of death. There were even some who fell a prey to total forgetfulness, so that they no longer knew themselves for what they were.

While many corpses lay unburied on the ground, heaped one upon another, yet carrion birds and beasts of prey either kept well away from them, repelled by the disgusting stench, or having tasted were stricken with a speedy death. In those days scarcely a bird was to be seen. No prowling predator emerged from the forests. Hosts of them were stricken with the plague and died. In particular, man's loyal servitors the dogs lay stretched in every street, battling vainly for the life that was dragged out of their limbs by the power of the pestilence.

Lonely funerals were raced without a mourner to the grave. No reliable remedy was found for general application. The treatment that had allowed one to draw the breath of life into his throat and remain a spectator of the starry vault proved in other cases a minister of death.

One especially distressing symptom was this: as soon as a man saw himself enmeshed in the malady, he lost heart and lay in despair as though under sentence of death. In expectation of death, he gave up the ghost there and then.

Without a pause the contagion of the insatiable pestilence laid hold of victim after victim, as though they had been fleecy sheep or horned cattle. One of the main factors that heaped death on death was this. Those whose excessive love of life and dread of death made them shrink from tending their own sick were punished before long by their own fatal negligence with a death as painful as it was disgraceful, unbefriended and destitute of aid. Those, on the other hand, who stood by the deathbed were overcome by contagion and the exertions imposed upon them by their sense of honour and the appealing voice of the enfeebled with its intrusive note of fretfulness. This, then, was the fate that overtook the finest characters.

Funeral parties would fling in one corpse upon another, in haste to dispose of their charges. Then back they would go, exhausted with tears and lamentation. Many were driven by sorrow to the sick-bed. The times were such that not a soul could be found untouched by death or sickness or mourning.

Meanwhile shepherd and herdsman and the sturdy pilot of the curved plough were among the victims. Within the cottage, body lay heaped on body, consigned to death by penury and pestilence together. Sometimes you might see the lifeless bodies of parents stretched above lifeless children, or children in turn gasping out their lives above prostrate parents. To no small extent the affliction was imported from the countryside into the city by the concentration there of the plague-stricken peasantry from every district, who crowded lanes and lodgings. Here, crammed within stifling walls, death piled high his heaps of victims. Along the roadside by the drinking fountains sprawled the bodies, prostrated and bowled over by thirst, of multitudes in whom the breath of life had been choked by too welcome water. Exposed in streets and public places you might see many a wasted frame with limbs half lifeless, begrimed with filth and huddled under rags, dying in squalor with nothing to cover the bones but skin, well-nigh buried already in loathsome sores and dirt. Every hallowed shrine of the gods had been tenanted by death with lifeless bodies – yes, all the temples of the Heavenly Ones, which their overseers had filled with guests, were left occupied by crowds of corpses. In this hour reverence and worship of the gods carried little weight: they were banished by the immediacy of suffering.

The mode of burial that had hitherto always been in vogue was no longer practised in the city. The whole nation was beside itself with terror. Each in turn, when he suffered bereavement, put away his own dead as circumstances permitted. Many unpleasant expedients were inspired by indigence and the suddenness of the event. Men would fling their own kinsfolk amid violent outcry on the pyres built for others and set torches to them. Often they shed much blood in these disputes rather than abandon their dead.